Modern Writers

The 'Modern Writers' series

Other titles in this new series of short guides to contemporary international writers:

David Timms

Philip Larkin

PHILIP LARKIN

Oliver & Boyd
Edinburgh

Oliver & Boyd

Croythorn House
23 Ravelston Terrace
Edinburgh EH4 3TJ

A Division of Longman Group Limited

0 05 002654 2 Hardback
0 05 002653 4 Paperback

Printed in Great Britain by
Cox & Wyman Limited,
London, Fakenham and Reading

Contents

Acknowledgements

Acknowledgements are due to Faber and Faber, Ltd., for permission to quote from *The North Ship*, *The Whitsun Weddings*, *Jill* and *A Girl in Winter*; to The Marvell Press for permission to quote from *The Less Deceived*; and to Philip Larkin himself for generously allowing me to quote from uncollected poems. I should also like to thank Anthony Thwaite for his assistance. I am indebted to some of my colleagues: to Paris Leary for his valuable suggestions while the book was in typescript, and to Ian Hilson for helping me with proofs, and preventing me from committing several blunders. Finally, I am particularly grateful for the help and encouragement of G. S. Fraser and Miss M. M. B. Jones: they are in large measure responsible for anything that may be found valuable in this study.

D.T.

Abbreviated titles by which Philip Larkin's works are cited in References

A.G.W. = *A Girl in Winter*
T.L.D. = *The Less Deceived*
T.N.S. = *The North Ship*
T.W.W. = *The Whitsun Weddings*

1 Philip Larkin and the Movement

'Philip Larkin is the best poet England now has. And that is not said with the intonation with which R. A. Butler once described Harold Macmillan as "the best Prime Minister we have".' Christopher Ricks, reviewing Larkin's most recent collection of poems, *The Whitsun Weddings* (1964) for the *New York Review of Books*, went on to claim for Larkin a status comparable to Andrew Marvell's. Both poets are 'minor', perhaps, but if we use that term in the cases of such poets as Larkin and Marvell, we are left with no terminology for the bulk. 'Minimal?' Ricks conjectures.

If Larkin is minor, then it must only be because of the small size of his body of work: he has published only four collections of verse. The first, *The North Ship* (1945), though it contains some good poems, and is certainly worth detailed consideration, is perhaps more interesting as the early work of someone who became a very good poet indeed than for its intrinsic merits. Of the second, *XX Poems* (1951), privately printed in a limited edition of one hundred in Belfast, only the thirteen poems later reprinted in the third collection, *The Less Deceived* (1955) and 'Waiting for breakfast while she brushed her hair', added to the second (1966) edition of *The North Ship*, are generally available. This means that Larkin's poetic reputation rests on less than one hundred poems: sixty-one from *The Less Deceived* and *The Whitsun Weddings*, and a few more not yet collected.

Larkin is not only a poet: he has written two fine novels, *Jill* (1946) and *A Girl in Winter* (1947). His penetrating and witty literary criticism makes one wish he wrote more—unless it took up time he would otherwise write poems in—and he has also contributed a regular column on jazz to the *Daily Telegraph*. But it is certainly as a poet that he is chiefly valued, and if the slight quantity of his published work prevents us from giving him the highest status, it does not prevent us from considering individual poems major achievements. In 1959, G. S. Fraser called 'Church Going', from *The Less Deceived*, 'possibly the one great poem written by a young English poet in the last ten years.'

Though Fraser is himself a good poet, he is best known as a literary critic, and the other authority I have quoted, Professor Ricks, is an eminent scholar. Both Fraser and Ricks are university lecturers, but in an age when poetry is largely an academic pursuit—as early as 1927, Robert Graves and Laura Riding in *A Survey of Modernist Poetry* could point to this fact—Larkin's verse can be, and is, appreciated by a very wide range of readers. This is not to say that Larkin's poems are slight or even simple: they are often complex, but never unnecessarily obscure. He has made his intentions clear, having praised Kipling and Housman for establishing a direct relationship with a wide reading public; and he has insisted that the audience at which he directs his poetry is that audience which reads poetry because it wants to, not that which reads it because it has to. And it seems that a great many people do want to read Larkin's poems. *The Less Deceived* was first published as a subscription issue of 300 copies, but even though its author was little known at the time, its merits were soon recognised, and it went through three printings in its first nine months. 3,800 copies of *The Whitsun Weddings* were sold within six months of publication.

Larkin has also been praised extensively by fellow poets. In a recent (1972) broadcast of tributes to Larkin on his fiftieth birthday, W. H. Auden called him 'a master of the English language'. Roy Fuller, who, like Auden, has been Professor of Poetry at Oxford, also recorded his admiration of Larkin's work in this broadcast, as did Larkin's distinguished, and very different contemporary Ted Hughes. Even if Anthony Thwaite, George Macbeth, Philip Hobsbaum and Douglas Dunn had not openly recorded Larkin's importance in the formation of their own styles, we should be able to read it in their work, as much as we are able to see Larkin's debt to Hardy in his own. Larkin has been explicitly approved by academics, and implicitly approved by the wider public, which buys his books; he has been praised by at least one great poet, and has been an important influence on several younger, good ones. But perhaps the most significant recognition of Larkin's stature was made by the Oxford University Press, in asking him to edit an *Oxford Book of Twentieth-Century English Verse* to succeed Yeats's *Oxford Book of Modern Verse* of 1936.

The high reputation Larkin has achieved has been won almost despite the poet himself. That he writes so little—about four poems a year, he has suggested, 'of which one is no good'[1]—is part of a more general tendency to keep himself away from public notice, and to eschew the popular image of the poet. His life has had none of the dramatic incident of Yeats's, say, or Dylan Thomas's; it has been determinedly provincial.

Larkin was born in Coventry on 9 August 1922, the same year as Kingsley Amis and Donald Davie, writers who were later associated with him in the group that came to be known as 'the Movement'. Like most of the other Movement poets, Larkin came from a professional, middle class background, his father being City Treasurer for Coventry between 1922 and 1944. Larkin has described his family as 'solid': 'everybody worked. No question about it. It was immoral not to work.'[2] Perhaps the family attitude prevailed upon Larkin, for he has always insisted that writing poetry is an activity he pursues in his spare time. However, this is not the attitude of a Congreve, based on a wish to be considered an amateur, a gentleman producing literature as an accomplishment; nor does he continue in his profession as librarian because of the insecurity of being a free-lance writer. Being a full-time poet, he considers, 'forces one too much to play the role of a poet'. Even as great a poet as Yeats ran this risk, he believes: 'there is quite a lot of his work where one feels he is deliberately hunting round for *something* to write a poem about.'[3]

Larkin's childhood was uneventful: in one poem he calls it 'a forgotten boredom',[4] and in another, he reflects on his childhood, recalling everything that did *not* happen, in a parody of the standard Portrait-of-the-Artist-as-a-Misunderstood-Young-Man sort of autobiographical novel:

1. Anon., 'Speaking of Writing XIII: Philip Larkin', *Times*, 20 February 1964, p. 16.

2. Philip Oakes, 'The Unsung Gold Medallist', *Sunday Times Magazine*, 27 March 1966, p. 65.

3. 'Speaking of Writing XIII: Philip Larkin', p. 16.

4. 'Coming', *T.L.D.*, p. 17.

> And here we have that splendid family
> I never ran to when I got depressed,
> The boys all biceps and the girls all chest,
> Their comic Ford, their farm where I could be
> 'Really myself.'[5]

From 1930 to 1940 Larkin attended King Henry VIII School, Coventry, one of two direct-grant grammar schools in the city. It seems he had little use for his schooling. In an article contributed to a short-lived Coventry arts magazine, *Umbrella*, on the subject of his years in Coventry, he refers to the times he had to spend at school as 'tiresome interruptions' of his reading. 'I was very stupid,' he reflected, 'until I could concentrate on English.' He read a great deal during his school years, being fortunate in that his father liked books. At home, as well as copies of the most important works of English literature, there were collections of the contemporary authors his father liked most. These included such figures as Huxley, Lawrence and Katherine Mansfield, who were considered a little advanced by families of Larkin's class at that time.

During his years at school, Larkin wrote extensively. Pieces appeared in the school magazine, the *Coventrian*, but these were apparently only a small part of a greater output: 'I wrote ceaselessly . . . now verse, which I sewed up into little books, now prose, a thousand words a night after homework.' Even then, it seems, business came first. The poems and stories that appear in the school magazine are interesting. As a schoolboy, Larkin seems to have made a speciality of the prose dramatic monologue, and we might note that some of his best known, and best, poems are dramatic monologues. Incidents usually revolve around the inept performance of some routine domestic job, which causes increasing exasperation in the speaker as he bungles it. As in the novels of his friend of later years, Kingsley Amis, objects seem to be malign forces, conspiring to frustrate the hero, and their intractability provokes violent anger. They are certainly controlled from what Amis was to call 'Bastards' H.Q.'. Obviously, we should not take these juvenile pieces too much into account in an assessment of the outlook and style of the mature poet, but

5. 'I Remember, I Remember', *T.L.D.*, p. 38.

they do indicate that Larkin had early formed some conception of the frustrations and disappointments of everyday life, and this informs much of his poetry. Amis's novels see its comic aspect, and so do these school pieces of Larkin's.

Larkin's early interest in writing seems to have been entirely self-generated. He remembers that none of his friends was interested in writing, and that 'no pipe-lighting dominie . . . casually slipped a well-worn volume into my hands as I was leaving his book-lined den'. The early poems seem to follow the natural curve of development described by T. S. Eliot in *The Use of Poetry and The Use of Criticism*: 'the usual adolescent course with Byron, Shelley, Keats, Rossetti, Swinburne.'[6] This is shown in their titles: 'Fragment from May', 'Summer Nocturne', 'Winter Nocturne'. Larkin later discovered Eliot's poetry, apparently, for those Eliotic great cats begin to stalk a familiar townscape of 'bare, windy streets'.

The last poem Larkin published in the *Coventrian*, 'Spring Warning', is very similar to 'Ultimatum', the first he published in a national periodical, and both follow closely the example of Auden in his 'In Time of War' sonnets. 'Ultimatum' had been sent to the *Listener* with three other poems, and Larkin apologetically admits that 'it was the one I had put in to make the others seem better'. J. R. Ackerley accepted 'Ultimatum', and it was published soon after Larkin went up to St John's College, Oxford, 'just when I was ready for an injection of self-esteem'.

At St John's, Larkin read English Literature and Language for three years. In completing his studies without interruption he was something of a rarity, as most undergraduates were called away from the university for war service after a fairly short time. Expecting this lot to be his, Larkin had gone up to Oxford a year early in order to spend as much time as possible at the University before having to join the forces, but in fact he failed his army medical after four terms, and so was able to complete the full nine.

The Oxford Larkin knew was quite different from that of before the war. Its portrait in *Jill* contrasts strongly with the Oxford in books by older writers: with Evelyn Waugh's of the 'twenties, say, as it is described in *Brideshead Revisited*, published

6. T. S. Eliot, *The Use of Poetry and the Use of Criticism*, London 1964, p. 33.

only a year before Larkin's first novel, or with Stephen Spender's slightly later one, as we see it in his autobiography, *World Within World*. The rationing of food, fuel and clothes meant that the flamboyance of a Harold Acton was impossible, and many traditional college social functions were suspended throughout the war. The social composition of the University was different in wartime. Edmund Crispin (pseudonym of Larkin's university friend, Bruce Montgomery) comments on this fact in his first detective novel, *The Case of the Gilded Fly* (1944), set in the Oxford of 1940: 'The average age of the college had been much reduced, and a sort of standard public-school prefect's common-room type had superseded the more adult eccentricities and individualities which had existed before the war.' Larkin has said of these years, 'at an age when self-importance would have been normal, events cut us ruthlessly down to size.'[7] What he was later to call in 'Send No Money' 'the hail/Of occurrence' was shaping the young man's life.

At least one of Larkin's teachers seems to have taken the same function upon himself. Larkin has recalled that the highest praise he was ever given by this man (whose name he cannot recall) was: 'Mr Larkin can see a point, if it is explained to him.' At the outset, Larkin's tutor was the Anglo-Saxon scholar Gavin Bone, but unfortunately he was not to see his pupil's academic distinction: he died in 1942, the year before Larkin took first-class honours. We cannot say how far Bone influenced Larkin, but it seems that they shared an unfashionable low opinion of T. S. Eliot's work. Larkin has often expressed his disapproval of obscurantism in Eliot's poetry; and in his *Anglo-Saxon Poetry* Bone slightingly refers to Eliot as 'an American critic'. The book was published in 1943, by which time, of course, Eliot enjoyed a reputation as a great poet, and had been a naturalised British subject for sixteen years.

At Oxford, Larkin's circle of friends included Alan Ross, Diana Gollancz, Edward du Cann and Bruce Montgomery. Larkin has described Montgomery as an 'intellectual epicurean' at this time, and this is fully borne out by the frequent references to literature, music and the other arts in *The Case of the Gilded Fly*. Montgomery seems to have acted as a catalyst to Larkin's own

7. Introduction, *Jill*, p. 12.

writing at this stage. The poet has said that during the time of their closest friendship, some three years in the mid-'forties, he 'wrote continuously as never before or since'. Certainly, these years were the most productive, in terms of quantity of published work, of Larkin's career: 1945 saw the publication of *The North Ship*; 1946, *Jill*; 1947, *A Girl in Winter*. Larkin also met John Wain at Oxford, though their friendship did not establish itself till later. Wain recalls in his autobiography, *Sprightly Running*, that at St John's, he and other undergraduates of his age were 'united in homage to Larkin'.[8]

By far the most important friendship Larkin made at Oxford was Kingsley Amis's. *Jill* is dedicated to Amis, as is *XX Poems*. 'Born Yesterday' was written for Amis's daughter, Sally. In his turn, Amis dedicated the brilliantly comic *Lucky Jim* to Larkin, and it is said that Jim Dixon is like Larkin in some respects: Jim's diatribe against 'filthy Mozart' echoes Larkin's then dislike of the composer. Amis's rather underrated poetry is sometimes like Larkin's in tone, though he lacks Larkin's scope as a poet, both in technique and subject matter. His novels reflect a similar world to that of Larkin's poems, though Amis concentrates on its comic aspects rather than its tragic ones, which engage Larkin more. These terms are relative in this context: a poem like Larkin's 'Sunny Prestatyn' is horrifying and comic at once. Similarly, Amis's latest novel, *Girl, 20*, is a funny but very bleak satire. Amis makes bitter humour from what he sees as the degeneration of our culture into a half-witted, destructive youth cult. At the end of the book, the only sympathetic young person we have met in its pages admits to the narrator that she is a heroin addict, certain to die within two years. This is a satisfying resolution of the fiction—though it hardly satisfies in any other sense—and it contrasts sharply with the simple solutions of Amis's first two novels, *Lucky Jim* and *That Uncertain Feeling*, which end with the easy removal of the hero from his uncomfortable environment.

Larkin seems to have thought of Amis, with his keen critical intelligence and his sharp eye for the phoney, as the ideal reader for his poetry. He has said that he wrote *The Less Deceived* 'under no particular influence except Kingsley's. I'd visions of showing

8. John Wain, *Sprightly Running*, London 1965, p. 188.

him things he would laugh at. It's a formidable experience to be laughed at by Kingsley.'[9]

John Wain reflects in *Sprightly Running* that Oxford's effect on him was so profound as to be deleterious. On Larkin it seems to have been less profound. When he lists his favourite poets, he mentions most often Hardy, Owen, Barnes, Betjeman and Stevie Smith, none of whom would have been considered in his degree courses, in which he studied literature written before 1830 only. And he has said that if he ever wrote an autobiography, it would have to begin when he was twenty-one, or even thirty-one, for nothing of any real importance happened to him before then.[10] He was twenty-one when he left St John's to take up a post in the public library of Wellington, a small town in Shropshire.

Taking this post, Larkin considers, 'seems to have determined the course of my life',[11] for he has remained a librarian. But he took up the career with a fair degree of indifference. When he considered what he should do, he applied more or less randomly for a number of jobs. The post at Wellington was his first offer, so he became a librarian almost by accident. It seems he has consistently lived the philosophy of his poems: in 'Dockery and Son', he says that what we are left with at the end of our lives is not necessarily what we wanted, but what 'something hidden from us chose'.

Larkin spent three years at Wellington, and the experience of working in a provincial public library gave him much of the material for *A Girl in Winter*. In 1944, a number of his poems were published in an anthology, *Poetry From Oxford in Wartime*, edited by William Bell. The Fortune Press had published the Bell anthology, and it was as a result of his appearance in this volume that Larkin was asked to submit a collection of his own work. *The North Ship*, which contained all the anthologised pieces plus some others, was published in 1945. The work of some well known poets had appeared under this imprint, Dylan Thomas and Roy Fuller among them. Later, the Fortune Press also published Kingsley Amis's first collection, *Bright November*. The

9. John Horder, 'Poet on the 8.15', *Manchester Guardian*, 20 May 1965, p. 9.
10. 'Poet on the 8.15', p. 9.
11. Anon., 'Four Young Poets—I: Philip Larkin', *Times Educational Supplement*, 13 July 1956, p. 933.

8

owner of the press was L. Caton. One L. S. Caton, it might be noted, makes brief appearances in Amis's novels as a rather obviously bogus academic, or editor of a suspect periodical. Caton also published *Jill*, one year later.

In 1946, Larkin left Wellington for a more academic library, taking up a post in what was then University College, Leicester. While he was in Leicester, *A Girl in Winter* was published by Faber and Faber. In 1950, Larkin moved to Queen's University, Belfast, as sub-librarian. He lived in Northern Ireland for five years, and wrote most of *The Less Deceived* there. *XX Poems* was published in 1951, and Larkin's attempt to distribute the one hundred copies seems to have been the only occasion on which he made strenuous efforts to bring his work to the attention of the literary world. Copies were sent to many of the leading literary figures of the time, but the pamphlet went almost entirely unnoticed. D. J. Enright, who reviewed it, and G. S. Fraser, who printed a selection of the poems in his 1953 anthology, *Springtime*, were the only recipients who publicly acknowledged its merit. If this implies a certain antagonism, it may have been caused by Larkin's putting 1d stamps on the packages when the postage had just been increased to 1½d. The experience of having made no impact whatsoever with his poems must have made him disinclined to press his collections in the future.

But it is more likely that the lack of attention paid to *XX Poems* was owing to the fact that it was not poetically fashionable. Larkin was already writing in the mood and style of the Movement: half the poems of *The Less Deceived* appeared previously in *XX Poems*, and at least one, 'Wedding Wind', was written as early as 1946. Of course, when the poems were published in the later collection, and a more controlled, phlegmatic and formal style was preferred, the poems received a much warmer reception.

Larkin has been considered by many to be the best of the Movement poets. A. Alvarez has said that Larkin embodies 'everything that was best in the Movement and at the same time shows what was finally lacking'.[12] I cannot agree with Alvarez, partly because I think Larkin does not share the faults of the Movement, and partly because Larkin's poetry does not seem

12. A. Alvarez, 'Poetry of the Fifties in England', in *International Literary Annual No. 1*, ed. John Wain, London 1958, p. 99.

to me to be so typical of that produced by the Movement that it may be picked out to epitomise its virtues. None the less, Larkin is so often considered in the context of the Movement that a knowledge of its chief characteristics is important background material to criticism of his poetry.

The chief poets of the Movement all contributed to Robert Conquest's anthology, *New Lines* (1956). They comprised Conquest himself, Philip Larkin, Donald Davie, Thom Gunn, John Holloway, Kingsley Amis, John Wain, D. J. Enright and Elizabeth Jennings. Conquest's was not the first Movement anthology: Enright had edited *Poets of the 1950's*, published in Tokyo in 1955, which included all the *New Lines* poets but Gunn; and earlier still, in 1953, G. S. Fraser and Iain Fletcher had edited an eclectic anthology called *Springtime*. *Springtime* included all the *New Lines* poets but Holloway and Conquest, as well as other young poets who were writing in the Movement style, notably Jonathan Price, Anthony Thwaite, George Macbeth and, perhaps surprisingly, in view of his present ideas on Movement poetry, A. Alvarez.

The Movement was not solely a poetic enterprise. In fact, it was first associated with novels rather than poems, particularly Amis's *Lucky Jim* (1954), John Wain's *Hurry on Down* (1953), and Iris Murdoch's *Under the Net* (1954). These three are often misleadingly grouped together. Though Amis's Jim Dixon has been considered the first 'Angry Young Man' of fiction, this doubtful accolade should surely go to Charles Lumley, of *Hurry On Down*. He and Jake Donaghue, of *Under the Net*, are early 'drop-outs': both highly educated, they cannot accept the sort of life for which their education was supposed to fit them, and so they take menial jobs. Lumley becomes a window-cleaner, and Donaghue a hospital porter, just as Jimmy Porter in John Osborne's *Look Back in Anger* keeps a sweet-stall. Jim Dixon, though he finds his superiors contemptible in the extreme, wants very much to make permanent his temporary post as university lecturer—at least, this is what he wants until something better turns up opportunely in the end. Much of the comedy in the book arises from Jim's wanting to tell his Professor just what he thinks of him, but being unable to do so for fear of jeopardising his job. Dixon, aware of the shortcomings of his society yet anxious to secure a place in it, is a characteristically Movement figure, and the others are not. The Movement writers would have frowned at such a grand gesture as 'chucking up' the job. Kingsley Amis illustrates this with reference to church parades while he was in the army. 'It was a point of honour with my generation,' he has said, 'never to opt for the slightest inconvenience on conscientious grounds of this kind. We let the army have its way and put "CE" on our identity discs, and were rather sophisticated with the occasional militant who insisted on "AGN[nostic]" or "N[o] R[eligion]".'[13]

The Movement poets had been publishing their work in the *Spectator*, and in the pamphlets published by Oscar Mellors's Fantasy Press. Larkin published such a pamphlet in 1954, *Fantasy Press: Pamphlet 21*. Some had had collections published in limited editions by the Reading University School of Art. The Movement did not receive its name, however, until 1954, when an anonymous writer published a piece in the *Spectator* entitled 'In the Movement'. The writer recognised that the composition of the group was unstable, but mentioned by name Donald Davie and Thom Gunn among poets, and Amis, Wain and Iris Murdoch among novelists.

> The Movement, as well as being anti-phoney, is anti-wet; sceptical, robust, ironic, prepared to be as comfortable as possible in a wicked, commercial, threatened world which doesn't look, anyway, as if it's going to be changed much by a couple of handfuls of young English writers.[14]

Besides enumerating some of the features of the Movement, this short quotation illustrates them. Movement writers tried to return to a diction that was recognisably that in which they spoke, a diction that eschewed the high-flown in favour of the colloquial. Here, it is illustrated in 'anti-phoney . . . anti-wet'. They maintained a wordly-wise stance, and took an ironical view of experience: we may see this irony—here rather

---

13. Kingsley Amis, 'On Christ's Nature', in *What Became of Jane Austen? And Other Questions*, London 1970, p. 212.

14. Anon., 'In the Movement', *Spectator*, 1 October 1954, p. 400.

heavy-handed—in the reference to 'this wicked, commercial world'. Sometimes this became a cynicism that smacked of self-pity: the world 'doesn't look, anyway, as if it's going to be changed much by a couple of handfuls of young English writers'.

In his introduction to *New Lines*, Robert Conquest suggests that the most important literary influence on the Movement was George Orwell. Certainly these poets followed Orwell's injunctions for clarity and straightforwardness of statement. They were also like Orwell in refusing to accept uncritically political or religious ideologies; only Elizabeth Jennings professed a faith: she is a Roman Catholic. Though in its formal strength and clarity of statement it was a return to the practice of Robert Graves and the school of Auden, the Movement would have none of Graves's 'White Goddess' poetic theories, nor the 'thirties poets' commitment to sweeping, revolutionary politics.

This aspect of the Movement is sometimes rather facilely explained as a loss of confidence after the departure of Auden and Isherwood for America in 1939. Perhaps this was a factor, but it seems more likely that the lack of 'commitment' was due to a certain cosy satisfaction with the social situation after the war. Until Suez and Hungary in 1956, British intellectuals were more or less content with Welfare State Britain. There was full employment, and though many foods were scarce, prices were controlled —restaurants were prohibited from charging more than five shillings for a *table d'hôte* meal, for instance. The political atmosphere was a leftish-rightness and rightish-leftness, which came to be known as 'Butskellism'. The war itself had begun to narrow social divisions, and the process was furthered by the 1944 Education Act, which gave working-class children the opportunity of an education to match their talents—in theory, at least. Edward Shils, an American academic visiting Britain, could report in *Encounter* in 1955: 'Never has an intellectual class found its society and its culture so much to its satisfaction.'

Like Jim Dixon, the intellectuals of the Movement's generation were ready to criticise vigorously the personalities within the Establishment, but had no real objection to it as a system. Movement figures like Amis, Wain and Alvarez attacked an older generation they considered phoney (much as Jim lampooned Professor Welch), but were quite ready to take over the important reviewing posts the 'phonies' vacated (Jim would himself have liked a senior university post).

A. Alvarez has diagnosed a set of 'negative feedbacks'[15] in twentieth-century poetry, which have produced the different modes of succeeding decades. As far as the Movement was concerned, the 'negative feedback' in question was a reaction against what he called the 'drum-rolling forties'. Poetry written in that decade, Alvarez suggested, was characteristically marked by its 'blockage against intelligence': the poets of the 'forties, with Dylan Thomas as their guide, had reacted against the cleverness of Auden and his followers in the 'thirties.

However, looking back on the 'forties, the poets we remember are figures like Keith Douglas, killed in the war, Sidney Keyes, also killed, or poets stationed in the Middle East during the war, like Lawrence Durrell, Terence Tiller and Bernard Spencer. Roy Fuller and Kathleen Raine also come to mind. None of these can be said to be imitators of Dylan Thomas. Even in the over-maligned 'New Apocalypse' group of poets which, I imagine, Alvarez had chiefly in mind, there were several good poets, like G. S. Fraser and Vernon Watkins, about whom it would be a travesty to say that they had 'a blockage against intelligence'. Moreover, it was during the 'forties that the real importance of such poets as Robert Graves and Edwin Muir began to be recognised. Three of Eliot's *Four Quartets* were published during the decade.

Alvarez went on to simplify the nature of the Movement—and Larkin's achievement in particular—in as drastic a way as he had that of the poetry of the 'forties. In the essay in which his views are expressed most fully, 'Beyond the Gentility Principle', which introduces the 1962 anthology, *The New Poetry*, he is speaking as a champion of certain poets he has called 'extremist' (though these writers, notably Robert Lowell, Sylvia Plath, John Berryman and Ted Hughes, knew each other, they did not write as a group) and it may be that any critic or poet who writes as a spokesman in this way needs to simplify literary history in order to emphasise the difference and importance of the poets he is trying to publicise. To the extent that young poets

15. A. Alvarez, 'Beyond the Gentility Principle', in *The New Poetry*, 2nd edition, Harmondsworth 1965, p. 21.

who are conscious of wishing to write in a new way are as likely as young critics to mythologise literary history like this, Alvarez was right to identify the Movement as a simple swing against the romanticism that was one aspect of some 'forties poetry. Thus, John Wain, in an article on contemporary British poetry for the American journal *Sewanee Review* in 1957, traced the course of twentieth-century British poetry through the same landmarks as Alvarez (and was taken to task by John Lehmann in the subsequent issue for the simplifications he perpetrated).

The earliest important critical statement of the Movement was also by John Wain. His article on the poetry of William Empson for *Penguin New Writing* in 1949[16] was both implicitly and explicitly a rejection of 'forties romanticism. Wain distinguished Empson's poetry from that of his contemporaries, Auden, Day Lewis and Spender, for its intellectual and formal strength. Too often, complained Wain, the metaphors employed by the 'pylon poets' of the 'thirties were introduced to give a contemporary flavour and nothing more. Empson followed the example of Donne, with all the intellectual subtlety that implies: his metaphors are not embellishment, but pivots upon which poems turn. But if Empson's poetry is intellectually stronger than his contemporaries', it shows up the flaccidity of the poetry of Dylan Thomas's imitators with an even more glaring light. Wain commended Empson's 'strong, almost perverse, desire to follow the argument wherever it leads the poem', and reflected that if Empson's practice were once more to become fashionable (as it did, in fact), the current 'punch-drunk, random, "romantic" scribblers' would find themselves very much out of favour.

Though it did not have the direct influence of John Wain's article, which encouraged many young poets to imitate Empson, I believe the central critical document of the Movement to be Donald Davie's *Purity of Diction in English Verse* (1952). It was certainly the theoretical backbone for his own early verse. The book was largely a study of the late Augustans: Goldsmith, Collins, Cowper, and, above all, Johnson. These poets, said Davie, were not concerned with innovation in language, but with renovation: with revivifying the metaphors of their predecessors,

16. John Wain, 'Ambiguous Gifts: Notes on the Poetry of William Empson', reprinted in *Preliminary Essays*, London 1957, pp. 169–80.

the great poets of the Augustan age, Pope and Dryden, which had degenerated into cliché in the verse of their imitators. (I am reminded here of John Wain's description of the Movement as an *avant garde* that was a rear-guard.[17]) The late Augustans' poetry was 'chaste'; it had 'strength', achieved through 'judgement and taste'. T. S. Eliot had said that poetry should have the virtues of good prose, and this poetry had them. It was a good model for new poets, Davie held.

He suggested, however, that the stable state of the conversational English in the poet's immediate circle at that time was necessary to the writing of poetry of this kind: Johnson's diction is the diction of the conversation in Mrs Thrale's drawing-room, and of her letters. Such poetry was no longer possible when the society that produced it, and for which it was written, began to break up. Thus, when Byron wanted to create an ironic, urbane tone for *Don Juan*, he could not do so by employing a 'pure' diction, for its conversational model was no longer current. He had to go to an extreme of 'impurity', therefore, and use a diction that vacillated wildly between one model and another, in order to achieve his ironic effect.

Now it seems to me that the society of the Movement poets in the first half of the 'fifties was in a similar position to that described by Davie. As many critics remarked on the publication of *New Lines*, the Movement was a very socially homogeneous group. Almost all the poets came from the professional middle classes, the only exception being Robert Conquest. Most had been educated at grammar schools, and had then gone up to Oxford or Cambridge to read English. Most had gained very good degrees, and had remained in the academic world. Wain, Amis, Enright, Holloway and Davie have all been university teachers of literature for some of their careers, and Conquest has done some teaching in an American university. Having left Cambridge, Gunn went to America to continue his studies under Yvor Winters at Stanford University. Larkin is a librarian, and Miss Jennings was one.

The Movement poets all 'spoke the same language'. In a sense, they were writing poetry for each other, or at least, for people

17. John Wain, 'English Poetry: the Immediate Situation', *Sewanee Review*, LXV (Summer 1957), p. 353.

very much like themselves. Their work was first published in limited editions by small private presses, and so was aimed not at the general public, but at the restricted, probably academic audience, which was the only one likely to buy poetry in limited editions. The audience, in fact, was very much like the poets. I think it is true to say that there was no such homogeneity in the 'thirties. The best known poets did come from similar backgrounds, social and educational; they tended to get poor degrees, where the Movement poets tended to get good ones; but the poets were quite unlike their audience. There could be no common background for ideological reasons: the poets of the 'thirties directed their poetry downwards, in a sense. Their form of address was characteristically not the first person but the second: 'you', the revolutionaries in Spain, the industrial workers in England, not 'we'. Ironically, in this way they semantically cut themselves off from the people they were trying to associate themselves with. And of course, those poets of the 'forties against whom the Movement poets were reacting had little homogeneity of any kind, social, educational, or even ethnic. Tambimuttu, editor of their chief organ, *Poetry (London)*, was a Ceylonese Tamil. Their exemplar was Dylan Thomas, a Welshman. The war meant that they were separated even geographically.

The Movement poets' sceptical, empirical attitudes, their unwillingness to indulge in large gestures, their concern for formal strength and elegance, and their wish to return to a poetic diction that had a vital relationship with the spoken language were without doubt good purgatives for many of the excesses of the more romantic forties poetry. But this very quality of guardedness also underlay their faults. 'At Dachau Yeats and Rilke died,'[18] Donald Davie memorably wrote; and in a different poem he stated the consequence: 'A neutral tone is nowadays preferred.'[19] The very enormity of some of the public events with which these poets grew up might have made any pronouncement on them seem lame. In any case, the British had gone to war and defeated Hitler—the people, poets among them, had done enough, perhaps. After the war politics were decent

18. Donald Davie, 'Hawkshead and Dachau in a Christmas Glass. An Imitation', *Brides of Reason*, Oxford 1955, p. 34.

19. 'Remembering the Thirties', *Brides of Reason*, p. 26.

if dull, unsuitable for treatment in the ode or satire, and certainly uninspiring. But even when there were stirring public events to write about, like Suez and Hungary, the Movement poets kept quiet. I take this reluctance to write about public affairs as evidence of a regrettable tendency rather than a particular fault: limiting *a priori* what it was permissible to write about meant that a great deal of Movement poetry lacked nutrition and variety. Kingsley Amis indicated this with characteristic directness in a short preface to a selection of his poems printed in Enright's *Poets of the 1950's*. 'Their great deficiency,' Amis observed of his contemporaries, 'is meagreness and triviality of subject-matter: nobody wants any more poems on the grander themes for a few years, but at the same time nobody wants more poems about philosophers or paintings or novelists or art galleries or mythology or foreign cities or other poems.'[20]

The two central Movement anthologies, *New Lines* and *Poets of the 1950's*, do contain too many poems about foreign cities. Such poems seem only one remove from the 'tepid nature poetry' about which Enright complains in the introduction to his anthology. Bernard Bergonzi has observed that twenty-five per cent of the poems in *New Lines* contain the words 'poet', 'poem', or 'poetry'.[21] Of course, the experience of writing poetry is as valid an experience to put in a poem as the well-known selection that T. S. Eliot lists in his essay 'The Metaphysical Poets': falling in love, reading Spinoza, the smell of cooking, and the noise of the typewriter. But if twenty-five per cent of the poems in an anthology mentioned, say, the smell of cooking, we should begin to suspect that the poets represented in it were somewhat un-inventive. It is paradoxical, too, that a preference for plainness should be married to a rather narcissistic tendency to write poems about writing poetry.

Their insistence on disciplined form had its drawbacks. One asks for some variety in poetry, and grows bored with the neat quatrains of the early Davie or the *terza rima* of the early Wain. The English iambic pentameter is a line capable of almost endless variation, but too often the Movement poets ignored its possibilities in favour of a regular thump. With diction, too

20. Kingsley Amis, in *Poets of the 1950's*, ed. D. J. Enright, Tokyo 1955, p. 17.
21. Bernard Bergonzi, 'After the Movement', *Listener*, 24 August 1961, p. 285.

determined an avoidance of the 'poetic' sometimes resulted in bathos. Kingsley Amis's 'The Value of Suffering' describes the decline of a Prince to a beggar:

> Now, shaven head abased, sandalled feet slow,
> He roams the crumbled courts and speaks to none;

but when Amis comments on this fall, he resorts to the flat and inadequate locution at the beginning of this line:

> What a shame that a regal house must founder.[22]

John Holloway, insisting on the ordinary words 'snap' and 'flash' in 'The Minute', manages to mix two metaphors and stir in a third within four short lines:

> no wonder if
> The hidden inner weir should snap
> And lose its strong long-hoarded power
> All in a flash:[23]

There was also a slyness about some Movement verse, which was the unpleasant side of the ironic mode. John Wain's 'On Reading Love Poetry in the Dentist's Waiting Room' is an example of this, with its uncharitable laugh at some poets' ineptnesses, and its rather cheap sexual puns:

> Such penetration how could she refuse?
> She writes here that she paid him love for love.
> The world was all before them where to choose
>
> Where gently as the wing-beats of a dove
> He should conduct her to the sacred cave,
> And wander in her like an orange grove.[24]

22. Kingsley Amis, 'The Value of Suffering', *A Case of Samples*, London 1956, p. 38.

23. John Holloway, 'The Minute', in *New Lines*, ed. Robert Conquest London 1956, p. 11.

24. *Poets of the 1950's*, p. 99.

Perhaps this is symptomatic of a general lack of sympathy with the different that one sometimes feels in Movement verse. Wain was able to write this poem because he knew that those who read it would be those who would roughly share his attitudes and education: he assumes his reader's familiarity with Book XII of *Paradise Lost* in the third line I quote. If it were read by someone who wrote the kind of poem Wain satirises, then he or she (more likely the latter, it seems, from Wain's poem) would be angry, or, perhaps, miss the joke.

I believe that Larkin did not share these faults, partly because he is a man more able to sympathise with others, and partly because he writes his poetry not from a preconceived set of principles, but as a direct and personal response to particular experiences. Donald Davie's poetry, for instance, has changed radically as his theoretical concepts have altered; but Larkin's has remained much more constant. Larkin has never eschewed the great theme on principle, nor the heightened diction that is often necessary for its statement. We need only look at the final stanzas of 'Church Going' and 'The Whitsun Weddings' to see this. Until recently, he has not written on public events in his poetry, but he has insistently written on those themes that are of perennial importance: the conflict between what we are and what we can imagine ourselves to be, the destructive effects of time, suffering as it hurts, and as it matures us, the endlessly complex relationships between people, the urge to slough off what Yeats called 'all this complexity of mire and blood'.

Technically, Larkin is an extraordinarily various and accomplished poet, a poet who uses the devices of metre and rhyme for specific effects, not just because, in Robert Frost's phrase, he likes to play his tennis with a net. His language is never flat, unless he intends it to be so for a particular reason, and his diction is never stereotyped. He is always ready, like Thomas Hardy, to reach across accepted literary boundaries for a word that will precisely express what he intends: into archaism, as in the 'accoutred' of 'Church Going'; into Americanism, as in the 'store-bought clothes' of the recent 'How Distant'; into coarse colloquial, in such phrases as 'books are a load of crap' from 'A Study of Reading Habits'; and even into the extremely uncommon usages of another poet, as in the 'prinked' brasswork of the ships in 'Next Please', a word surely used in the sense in which Hardy uses it in 'Beeny Cliff', where the tops of waves are 'prinked' by the sun.

Larkin has a sympathy with the different that is lacking in the work of many of his Movement contemporaries. Amis would not feel what Larkin feels in 'Faith Healing' for the women who shake, 'moustached in flowered frocks'. He would make brilliant comedy out of it, but he could not feel Larkin's compassion. His attention would be riveted by the moustaches.

Most important, perhaps, Larkin's attention is not turned inwards upon himself and his art—at least, this is true of his poetry after *The North Ship*. Though, as I pointed out above, twenty-five per cent of the poems in *New Lines* use the words 'poem', 'poet' or 'poetry', Larkin's mature poems do not include any of those words. And this is true of all the poems of *The Less Deceived* and *The Whitsun Weddings*, not just the selection printed in *New Lines*: poetry is his medium, not his subject. The Movement was a valuable force, and from it emerged a body of excellent writing. But Larkin's poetry seems to me better and more important than what was generally produced. When *The Less Deceived* was reviewed in the *Times Literary Supplement* it was given the praise it deserved. '*The Less Deceived*', the reviewer considered, 'should establish Mr Philip Larkin as a poet of quite exceptional importance; he has a mature vision and the power to render it variously, precisely and movingly.'[25]

Like *The North Ship*, *The Less Deceived* was published without its being pressed on a publisher. The enterprising George Hartley, who ran the Marvell Press, which printed the excellent poetry magazine *Listen*, wrote to Larkin in Belfast showing interest in his poems. Early in 1955, Larkin sent to the Marvell Press a typescript entitled 'Various Poems'. Hartley persuaded Larkin to change his title, and the book became *The Less Deceived*, which was what 'Deceptions' was originally called. It took almost a year to print and bind, and during this year Larkin took up a post in the University at Hull, where he has remained.

It was only after the publication of *The Less Deceived* that Larkin's reputation began to establish itself. He continued to

25. Anon., 'Poetic Moods', *Times Literary Supplement*, 16 December 1955, p. 762.

write slowly, and it was almost nine years before his next collection, *The Whitsun Weddings*, was published by Faber and Faber.
This third book of poems consolidated Larkin's standing, winning
the Queen's Gold Medal for Poetry in 1965. In the same year as
The Whitsun Weddings appeared, *Jill* was reprinted by Faber, with
an introduction by Larkin, and in the following year *A Girl in
Winter* was reprinted for the second time. In 1966, a new edition
of *The North Ship* was published, also by Faber, and like *Jill*
it had an interesting and informative introduction by Larkin
himself.

Since 1961, Larkin has reviewed new jazz records for the *Daily
Telegraph*, and in 1970 Faber and Faber published a large
selection of his reviews in *All What Jazz?* Larkin's preferences
in jazz are as strongly stated as his preferences in literature.
Blues, the ethnic music of the American Negro, created spontane-
ously within the limits of a traditional but flexible form, and
directly expressing the needs, complaints and aspirations of a
suffering and oppressed people, is the staple and norm of authentic
jazz, Larkin believes. Modernism has distorted it so far as to
make it almost unrecognisable. Though I am not claiming that
Larkin's likes and dislikes in jazz—or in poetry—are determined
by social rather than aesthetic considerations, there is a parallel
between his beliefs about jazz and his poetic practice. He has
said that poetry is 'born of the tension between what [the poet]
non-verbally feels and what can be got over in common word-
usage to someone who hasn't had his experience or education or
travel-grant'.[26] In common with Dr Johnson, Larkin sees in
life 'much . . . to be endured and little to be enjoyed'; and like
the blues singer's art, Larkin's poetry mediates between this
experience and his audience. His forms are 'traditional' rather
than 'modern', though they are various, and unmistakably a
full response to contemporary life.

26. Philip Larkin, 'The Pleasure Principle', *Listen*, II (Summer-Autumn
1957), p. 29.

2   *The North Ship*

I stress that the remarks at the end of my last chapter apply to
Larkin's mature verse. Introducing the second (1966) edition of
his first book of poems, Larkin recalls the verdict of his friend
Vernon Watkins, who read *The North Ship* soon after its initial
publication. Though Watkins was encouraging, he gave some
oblique advice to the younger man by referring to his own
poems: 'Yesterday,' Watkins said, 'I destroyed about two
thousand poems that mean nothing to me now.' The poems in
The North Ship are juvenilia, and will not bear the very close
critical reading that is appropriate to Larkin's mature work; but
as one reviewer remarked on the publication of the second edition,
'the juvenilia of the best poets are always worth reading'. Besides,
set against *The North Ship*, the virtues of *The Less Deceived* and
The Whitsun Weddings may be seen more clearly.

Larkin himself lists three specific influences on his early poetry:
'Looking back, I find in the poems not one abandoned self but
several—the ex-schoolboy, for whom Auden was the only alternative to "old-fashioned" poetry; the undergraduate, whose work
a friend affably characterized as "Dylan Thomas, but you've a
sentimentality that's all your own"; and the immediately post-
Oxford self, isolated in Shropshire with a complete Yeats stolen
from the local girls' school.'[1] We can certainly see Auden in one
or two poems. 'Conscript', as the title suggests, is about becoming
involved in a war—certainly promising material for one who
wants to write like Auden:

> The ego's county he inherited
> From those who tended it like farmers; had
> All knowledge that the study merited,
> The requisite contempt of good and bad;[2]

1. Introduction, *T.N.S.*, p. 8.
2. *T.N.S.*, p. 16.

The sonnet is squarely based on the poems from Auden's *In Time of War*, even in its typographical arrangement: it is split up into three quatrains and a couplet on the page, in a similar way to Auden's splitting up of his sonnets. The language has the rather cultivated toughness, and even a hint of the psychological jargon of Auden's early work. The friend was right—there is a sentimentality here, for Larkin's soldiers, and the method of his friend's conscription, are too much romanticised. Perhaps his is the enthusiasm of the man who believes in a cause, but is unable to fight to support it.

Dylan Thomas's influence is vestigial. Here, Larkin uses Thomas's trick of fusing two ideas together into a metaphor that surprises because it is completely inappropriate. Larkin sits in a railway carriage, watching a Polish airgirl speaking incomprehensibly to her companion:

> Hair, wild and controlled, runs back:
> And gestures like these the English oaks
> Flash past the windows of her foreign talk.[3]

The oaks flash past the windows, certainly; but there is no sense, literal or metaphorical, in which her talk has 'windows'. Indeed, if her talk is 'foreign', it is presumably quite opaque to the listening poet. In another poem, Larkin uses the technique Thomas uses in 'In the Beginning':

> Life rose and spouted from the rolling seas,
> Burst in the roots, pumped from the earth and rock
> The secret oils that drive the grass.[4]

It is a technique of association: life began in the sea, and Thomas visualises the beginning of life as a tremendous waterspout, which reminds him of an oil gusher—and the oil will then 'drive the grass', as petrol drives an internal combustion engine. Again, the metaphor is startling, but inappropriate. We are only too aware today that the by-products of technology do the reverse of forcing

3. 'XII', *T.N.S.*, p. 24.
4. Dylan Thomas, 'In the Beginning', *Collected Poems 1934–1952*, London 1966, p. 20.

up grass. Larkin has a metaphor that works in the same way in poem XVIII:

> If grief could burn out
> Like a sunken coal,
> The heart would rest quiet,
> The unrent soul
> Be still as a veil;[5]

It seems that the poet has made an original and profound simile in the fifth line. But in fact, this effect is spurious. The associating link is between lines four and five, the portentous Biblical reference to the torn veil in the temple. The reader's mind makes the association the poet's must have done, between 'unrent' and 'veil', and it is this essentially irrelevant association that creates the shock of originality or profundity. Like electricity, the shock runs to earth through the first conductor it touches, and that is the other element in the simile, 'as still as a veil'. If we consult the evidence of our senses, there is nothing particularly still about a veil: the simile has no power whatever out of its context.

Despite Larkin's admission, even so sensitive a reader as Anthony Thwaite has said that he can find no trace of Dylan Thomas in *The North Ship*. I think he is wrong, as I have pointed out above; but it is certainly justifiable to say that there is little evidence of Dylan Thomas. Its scantiness is surprising in view of the reverence in which Thomas was held by young poets at the time of the publication of *The North Ship*. In a critical work on contemporary poetry published in 1942, *Auden and After*, Francis Scarfe described the New Apocalypse as 'a new Romantic movement, less irresponsible than Surrealism and Dadaism, less frantic than that represented by Lawrence, less "literary" than that of Eliot and Pound, less restrained than the Romanticism of Herbert Read, less recondite than that of Laura Riding'.[6] For this group of poets, Scarfe considered, Dylan Thomas was a 'god'. As Larkin says in his introduction to *The North Ship*, 'the principal poets of the day—Eliot, Auden, Dylan Thomas, Betjeman—were all

5. *T.N.S.*, p. 30.
6. Francis Scarfe, *Auden and After*, London 1942, p. 181.

speaking out loud and clear'; but it is certainly true that to young poets the voice of Dylan Thomas could be heard well above the rest. It is an interesting and important negative fact that a book of poems by a young poet should contain so little trace of the work of the greatest influence on other young contemporary poets. The poems of the others represented in *Poetry From Oxford in Wartime* are in nearly all cases stamped with Thomas's mark—why not Larkin's?

The answer is not that the young poet was not impressionable, or that he had already found his characteristic and unique voice: Yeats was a very strong and obvious influence on his early work, as I shall show below. The reason is rather that Larkin was never seduced by fashionable notions of what a poet should be, or how he should write. As I suggested above, with regard to the reception of the poems from *XX Poems* that were reprinted in *The Less Deceived*, taste had to catch up with Larkin, rather than Larkin conform to taste.

Eliot, having charted the development of a young poet through the influence of the Romantics, says that in the succeeding stage, 'the poetry of a single poet, invades the youthful consciousness and assumes complete possession for a time'.[7] In Larkin's case, the single poet was Yeats. In Larkin's last year at Oxford, 1943, Vernon Watkins was invited to speak to the English Club, and he spoke most enthusiastically about Yeats. After his lecture, he distributed to those sitting at the front of the audience some of his (at that time) rare copies of Yeats's late verse. Larkin took it upon himself to collect up Watkins's books and return them to him—but not before he had himself conceived a passion for the great Irish poet. 'As a result,' he says, 'I spent the next three years trying to write like Yeats, not because I liked his personality or understood his ideas but out of infatuation with his music (to use the word I think Vernon used). In fairness to myself it must be admitted that it is a particularly potent music, pervasive as garlic, and has ruined many a better talent.'[8] In this connection, we may note the opinions of Keats and T. S. Eliot on Milton, that, paradoxically, a great poet may be a most dangerous influence on young writers.

7. *The Use of Poetry and the Use of Criticism*, p. 34.
8. Introduction, *T.N.S.*, p. 9.

Though we can spot Auden and Dylan Thomas only here and there in *The North Ship*, Yeats is everywhere. The edition of Yeats Larkin knew well was the 1933 *Collected Poems*, which includes his work only up to *Words for Music Perhaps*. Larkin is obviously most impressed by the later poems in the collection, from the poems of *The Tower* onwards. But though he borrows the idiom of these great poems, he shows that his attitudes are closer to those of the younger, *fin de siècle* Yeats.

Poem XX shows how completely Larkin assimilated the mode of Yeats's middle period. The reflections and statements in the poem cluster round two separate groups of individuals the poet sees, much as those in the second part of Yeats's 'The Tower' grow from his calling before his mind's eye images of characters he has known, or heard of, or himself created. Out walking in winter, Larkin sees a young girl enjoying herself with her friends in intensely physical activity, and he reflects that there would have been a time when at such a sight 'I should choke with powerless jealousies'; but this is no longer the case. Perhaps, he thinks, the hopes he once had of enjoying himself as she does have expired. But unexpectedly, and paradoxically, he has a powerful surge of emotion at seeing two ragged labourers clearing away snow. He realises that this is an analogue of his own situation: he must endure such grinding work, forging his 'explanatory rhymes', for it is only such shovel and spade work that:

> Builds up the crags from which the spirit leaps
> —The beast most innocent
> That is so fabulous it never sleeps;
> If I can keep against all argument
> Such image of a snow-white unicorn,
> Then as I pray it may for sanctuary
> Descend at last to me,
> And put into my hand its golden horn.[9]

The poem seems to me to grow from a close reading of three of Yeats's greatest poems: 'Sailing to Byzantium', 'The Tower' and 'A Dialogue of Self and Soul'. From 'The Tower', Larkin's

9. *T.N.S.*, p. 33.

poem borrows its narrative technique, and its metrical and stanzaic form—in fact, all three of Yeats's poems have this eight line stanza, which he used extensively in *The Tower*, but only the title poem of the collection has the same flexibility of line length as Larkin's—and from 'A Dialogue of Self and Soul' poem XX borrows its self-questioning manner and its rhyme scheme. 'Sailing to Byzantium' provides its property-basket of metaphors, and its central idea, that a poet makes up for the disappointments of his life through his art. Yeats declares:

> An aged man is but a paltry thing,
> A tattered coat upon a stick, unless
> Soul clap its hands and sing, and louder sing
> For every tatter in its mortal dress,[10]

The young poet feels that

> I can
> Never in seventy years be more a man
> Than now—a sack of meal upon two sticks.[11]

and that, like the 'two old ragged men', he must be 'content to wear a worn-out coat', until, through his poetry, the horn of plenty comes into his grasp.

Other poems take up the more rhythmic style of *Words for Music Perhaps*, with its short, dancing lines and portentous refrains. Compare the first stanza of 'Her Anxiety':

> Earth in beauty dressed
> Awaits returning spring.
> All true love must die,
> Alter at the best
> Into some lesser thing.
> *Prove that I lie.*[12]

with the first stanza of the first poem in *The North Ship*:

10. W. B. Yeats, 'Sailing to Byzantium', *Collected Poems*, 2nd edition, London 1950, p. 217.
11. *T.N.S.*, p. 32.
12. W. B. Yeats, *Collected Poems*, p. 297.

> All catches alight
> At the spread of spring:
> Birds crazed with flight
> Branches that fling
> Leaves up to the light—
> Every one thing,
> Shape, colour and voice,
> Cries out, Rejoice!
>   *A drum taps: a wintry drum.*[13]

These two poems, XX and I, show that in some of his early work, Larkin borrowed far more than the Yeatsian tone of voice. For XX he borrows Yeats's view of the poet: the man struggling with intractable materials, forced to choose 'perfection of the life, or of the work', and not both, forced into isolation in his tower, or on the crags he builds, for only there may his 'spirit leap'. For I, he borrows Yeats's view of time, of evolution and the second coming, his wheel another version of the Yeatsian gyre:

> Let the wheel spin out,
> Till all created things
> With shout and answering shout
> Cast off rememberings;
> Let it all come about
> Till centuries of springs
> And all their buried men
> Stand on the earth again.[14]

These poems are marvellous imitations. Of course, if they were indistinguishable from their originals, they too would be great poems; but they are not. What are their defects, then? It seems to me that their greatest single fault is their lack of particularity, which makes them insubstantial. Too often the young poet sketches a stock poetic landscape in an attempt to evoke a vague mood of ennui or melancholy rather than a feeling of a real object, situation, set of events, or state of mind. The wind is blowing in at least a third of the thirty-one poems in the volume

13. *T.N.S.*, p. 11.
14. *T.N.S.*, pp. 11–12.

as it stood when it was first published. When the time of day is mentioned, it is always day-break, and a cold, often rainy day-break at that. The young poet will never let objects stand as they are—he always romanticises or sentimentalises them. 'Ugly Sister', as its title suggests, is about a girl whose plainness has prevented her from being loved, but her response is philosophical:

> I will attend to the trees and their gracious silence,
> To winds that move.[15]

Such attitudes are ridiculed in a poem of Larkin's maturity, 'I Remember, I Remember', in which he recollects his own childhood, and says that he 'did not invent/Blinding theologies of flowers and fruits'.[16] In 'Nursery Tale', the speaker makes his own failures heroic, by comparing himself with a figure like someone from *The Cloister and the Hearth*, a horseman who arrives late at night at a house where he finds that though

> His place was set, there was no more
> Than one unpolished pewter dish, that bore
> The battered carcase of a carrion crow.[17]

The speaker's experiences are similar:

> So every journey that I make
> Leads me, as in the story he was led,
> To some new ambush, to some fresh mistake:

This is self-pity of a kind quite foreign to the mature writer. None of the poems has a recognisable locale, or familiar objects: rooms are lit by candles, not electric lights; when a stranger is set a meal, he is given 'loaves and wine'; when a man is conscripted, horsemen arrive for him, not green army trucks.

Perhaps the sentimentality of attitude is most evident in the love poems. Again, one never feels that a poem arises from a real set of circumstances, or that it is addressed to a real person. The

15. *T.N.S.*, p. 31.
16. *T.L.D.*, p. 38.
17. *T.N.S.*, p. 26.

loved one is never described. If we look back to Yeats's early poems, we find there no evocation of what the loved one—Maud Gonne, a real enough individual—actually looks like. There are many references to teeming hair and to heavy, dream-laden eyes, but that is as concrete as the description gets.

> And like a sunset were her lips,
> A stormy sunset on doomed ships;[18]

wrote the young Yeats. The simile is impossible to realise. At this stage, Yeats seems interested more in his own state of mind than in the object that ostensibly interests him. Similarly, in *The North Ship* it often appears that the speaker is trying to induce in himself a mood of rather maudlin melancholy, rather than to express his love, or its failure, or to understand it. One poem reads like a rather uninventive popular song, and turns on just the sort of verbal trick that such songs so often do:

> Is it for now or for always,
> The world hangs on a stalk?
>
> .   .   .
>
> Shine out, my sudden angel,
> Break fear with breast and brow,
> I take you now and for always,
> For always is always now.[19]

Other poems take the 'sophisticated', world-weary, 'The Party's Over' kind of view:

> Love, we must part now: do not let it be
> Calamitous and bitter. In the past
> There has been too much moonlight and self-pity:[20]

And in the present, we might add. Here again, Larkin is much more like the early Yeats, expressing none of the vital sexuality, whether despairing or exultant, that gives such pressure to Yeats's later love poems, and such concreteness:

18. 'The Wanderings of Oisin', *Collected Poems*, p. 409.
19. 'XXVIII', *T.N.S.*, p. 41.
20. 'XXIV', *T.N.S.*, p. 37.

A woman can be proud and stiff
When on love intent;
But Love has pitched his mansion in
The place of excrement;[21]

The young Larkin would have read poems of this kind, as well
as 'Sailing to Byzantium' and 'Among School Children'.

The North Ship shows that even at this age, Larkin was a poet
of great technical expertise. In some poems, he demonstrates his
ability to sound conversational within a tight formal framework,
an ability he was to develop further, in poems like "I Remember,
I Remember' and 'Lines On A Young Lady's Photograph
Album'. Poem II is a sonnet, and it contains these lines:

sunbeams are prodigal
To show you pausing at a picture's edge
To puzzle out the name, or with a hand
Resting a second on a random page—[22]

They might have come from his mature work, the feeling for the
iambic line is so sure. Even in this early work, one never suspects
that Larkin is tapping out his rhythms with his foot.

I have stressed Larkin's dependence on Yeats for many of the
poems in *The North Ship*, but there are many good poems that
are not at all imitative. Poem VII is about the way a natural
scene can be so splendid that it makes human worries and fears
seem of little consequence. The regularity and balance of the
lines in the first stanza make it sound like a hymn, praising natural
beauty:

The horns of the morning
Are blowing, are shining,

Subtle changes in the opening lines of the second stanza—their
shortening by an unstressed syllable in each, and the movement
of the caesura from the middle of the line—disrupt the hymnal

21. 'Crazy Jane Talks with the Bishop', *Collected Poems*, p. 295.
22. *T.N.S.*, p. 13.

rhythm, emphasising the incongruity of the speaker's disappointments and fears. The poem rejects the 'pathetic fallacy': such beauty is indifferent to our human emotions.

> Here, where no love is,
> All that was hopeless
> And kept me from sleeping
>   Is frail and unsure;
> For never so brilliant,
> Neither so silent
> Nor so unearthly, has
>   Earth grown before.[23]

The earth is 'silent', even though all the metaphors describing it in the first stanza had referred to loud musical instruments. The contradiction reinforces the poet's feeling that on this morning the earth is 'unearthly', transcendent. In poem XXX, too, Larkin speaks with an individual voice. As in poem II, he maintains an idiomatic style within a firm formal structure. It is a poem about someone he had loved, but there is no sentimentality of the 'Let there be no more moonlight and self-pity' variety. Again, the concluding lines, suggesting that his memory of the girl is no more than a kind of mental snapshot, which he might bring out to divert himself on cold winter evenings, might have been written in *The Less Deceived*.

These two poems, VII and XXX, also show what may be the most interesting thing about *The North Ship*, seen in the context of Larkin's work as a whole. Though he was not speaking in his authentic voice, and though he was to change his manner of illustrating them, the themes that have continued to occupy him were established in this first book. Poem VII is like the later 'Absences' in suggesting the contingency of humanity to nature. 'Whatever Happened' takes up the theme of poem XXX, that memory distorts the real character of events. Many poems in *The North Ship* are about the effects of time, a theme to which Larkin insistently returns throughout his work. Poem XXVI states the problem in the form of a Yeatsian epigram. The mature poet would not make quite so theatrical a statement, and would

23. *T.N.S.*, p. 18.

be concerned more about time's effect on people than on trees, perhaps.

> This is the first thing
> I have understood:
> Time is the echo of an axe
> Within a wood.[24]

Larkin may be remembering the end of *The Cherry Orchard* here. Other poems in *The North Ship* are about the way our lives so rarely turn out how we hoped they would—we fail so often, particularly in love. Some deal with loneliness: again, a characteristic theme of the later verse, where it is examined in a more complex fashion. Some themes are quite alien to the mature poetry, of course: the Larkin of *The Whitsun Weddings* would never wish his youth away as the speaker of poem XXIX does. More significant, the mature poet does not write about his own art, as the young one does. Frequent reference to the fact that the speaker of a poem is a poet is very characteristic of a young and self-conscious writer—but the trials of a poet as a poet are less interesting to us, perhaps, than the trials of a poet as a man.

Added to the thirty-one poems of *The North Ship* on its re-publication in 1966 was a poem from the 1951 *XX Poems*. The poem dates from the same time as the earliest pieces in *The Less Deceived*; that is, from about 1946. Larkin says in his introduction that he added the poem as a 'coda'. He claims that it is no better than the others—I disagree—but it 'shows the Celtic fever abated and the patient sleeping soundly'. The poet in poem XXXII has spent the night with a girl, and he stands looking out of the hotel window while she brushes her hair. At the sight of a dull scene, he reflects that what he sees is a 'Featureless morning', following a 'featureless night'. But he is suddenly overtaken by a feeling of joy, which seems to change the very appearance of the 'featureless' things he has seen outside: where the 'cobblestones were wet' in the first stanza, he now sees that 'the stones slept'; where the sky has been 'loaded . . ./Sunk as it was with mist down to the roofs', he now realises that 'the mist/Wandered absolvingly past all it touched'; where the 'rooms still burning their electric

24. *T.N.S.*, p. 39.

light' had been uninteresting, he now calls them 'pin-points of undisturbed excitement'. His attitude towards the girl had been indifference; but this sudden access of joy changes it:

> Turning, I kissed her,
> Easily for sheer joy tipping the balance to love.[25]

The last stanza generalises that a feeling of love, if it comes, comes like this one, unprompted and unpredictable. Or it may be that, paradoxically, such a feeling will come only after one assumes, as the speaker had, that it will not: 'Featureless morning, featureless night.'

> Are you jealous of her?
> Will you refuse to come till I have sent
> Her terribly away, importantly live
> Part invalid, part baby, and part saint?

The poem is a 'coda' to the others in *The North Ship* in the sense that it shows Larkin speaking in his authentic tone, abandoning those attitudes towards poetry and what is suitable for inclusion in it that had marred the earlier work. The poeticisms have gone: the rooms in the hotel where it is set are lit by electric light bulbs, not candles, and it has drainpipes and a fire escape. The setting is specific. Anthony Thwaite has suggested that we we may take the idea of the poem's being a coda more literally, and see the poem as being about writing poetry: 'One sees that what it turns into is an address to the Muse.'[26] By this reading, the last few lines, quoted above, pose the question: 'Will absorption in the girl and in the happiness she seems to bring stifle my poems?' I do not agree with this reading, although it seems a reasonable one at first sight. None of the other poems in *XX Poems*, and only one in both *The Less Deceived* and *The Whitsun Weddings* combined, deals with the subject of writing poetry; this is characteristic of *The North Ship*, but not of the post-1945 poems. However, many of the poems in *XX Poems* deal with love

25. *T.N.S.*, p. 48.
26. Anthony Thwaite, 'The Poetry of Philip Larkin', in *The Survival of Poetry: A Contemporary Survey*, ed. Martin Dodsworth, London 1970, p. 43.

and its vagaries, and at least one other deals with the topic of an unexpected access of happiness. Moreover, as Thwaite says, this poem establishes 'the new presence of Hardy'. The theme as I have read it, that it seems that we can only fully feel love towards someone when he or she has left us, would certainly suggest itself to someone writing under Hardy's influence. That great poet's love for his first wife, Emma Lavinia, was never felt more strongly nor expressed more poignantly than in the poems he wrote just after her death, the *Poems of 1912–13*, subtitled *Veteris Vestigia Flammae*. Just as for the speaker in poem XXXII, Hardy's love was not fully expressed until its object had been 'sent . . . terribly away'.

In this 'coda' to *The North Ship*, a good poem worth inclusion on grounds of sheer merit, not merely of history, Larkin shows that he is beginning to see himself in the context of the real world. His next two publications were novels, and it may be that this process of turning his attention outwards was assisted by writing in the more expansive form. For a novel, one needs furniture from the world outside, and people other than oneself, if only to fill the space.

3   *Jill* and *A Girl in Winter*

Larkin has written only two novels, *Jill* and *A Girl in Winter*, published in 1946 and 1947 respectively. In an interview in 1972 he said that between the completion of *A Girl in Winter* and that of the pamphlet, *XX Poems*, 'life was one long, dreary attempt to write a third novel',[1] and he now looks back somewhat nostalgically to the time when he was writing fiction. 'Up to 1950,' he said elsewhere, 'the novel seemed to me the more difficult, the more worthwhile thing to do, and it still does in the abstract.'[2] The last point is disputable, of course; but to keep to the concrete, it seems to me that the more worthwhile thing for Larkin to do is to write poems. He is certainly a better poet than novelist, on the evidence we have before us.

On the other hand, he is certainly a better novelist than he gives himself credit for. In the introduction to the second edition of *Jill*, published in 1964, he begs his reader's indulgence for his first novel, on the grounds of its being 'juvenilia'—it was written in 1943–4, when Larkin was twenty-one. And he has also said that his were 'not very good novels', that they were written 'not very successfully'. Neither novel needs any such apology. Bruce Montgomery, Larkin's close friend and contemporary at Oxford, reviewing the second edition of *Jill* for the *Spectator* under his pseudonym, Edmund Crispin, makes a balanced judgement on Larkin's first novel: 'Although *Jill* may have been a disregarded good book, it wasn't a disregarded early masterpiece.'[3] That applies to *A Girl in Winter*, too.

One American commentator, James Gindin, in his book on the contemporary novel, *Post-War British Fiction*, sees John Kemp,

1. Frances Hill, 'A Sharp Edged View', *Times Educational Supplement*, 19 May 1972, p. 19.
2. John Horder, 'Poet on the 8.15', p. 9.
3. Edmund Crispin, 'An Oxford Group', *Spectator*, 17 April 1964, p. 525.

the hero of *Jill*, as the precursor of a particular type of fictional hero better known in the novels of Kingsley Amis, John Wain and Iris Murdoch: the young man disorientated from his social class by his education. Larkin has disclaimed any sociological intent in this book, though he admits that Gindin's is 'fair trend-spotter's comment'.[4] It certainly seems to me that this is one of the less important aspects of the book. Larkin was not writing about the condition of society with respect to education and social class, but about a theme to which he often returns in his mature poetry: our tendency to make fantasies, and the dangers into which it leads us.

John Kemp is a working-class boy, the son of a retired police-man. He comes from a northern town, Huddlesford. At his grammar school, a young and rather cold English master, Higgins-like, cultivates John as an experiment. The result is that John, intelligent and hard-working, though quite passive, wins a scholarship to Oxford at the age of eighteen, in 1940. His passivity stems from an almost total lack of self-confidence and near-neurotic shyness. Travelling to Oxford on the train, he feels so embarrassed about eating in front of the other occupants of his carriage that he goes to the lavatory to eat his food, and then stuffs it out of the window when someone rattles the door.

It seems that John needs someone to imitate: his great fear is of being alone, of having nowhere to fit and no pattern to fit into. Having left his home, he is confronted at Oxford with two contrasting societies. One is Christopher Warner's. Christopher is a brash, over-confident young man with whom John shares rooms. He is John's opposite in every way, radically different in character and in social class. He has little intelligence and less industry, but all the traditional characteristics of the 'hearty': he is a sportsman, a drinker and a womaniser. His over-plus of social confidence makes him selfish: he does not worry about borrowing other people's possessions, or about eating their sparse, rationed food. Where John's deference to the wishes of others is painfully self-effacing, Christopher is always ready to manipulate his friends to his own advantage. Christopher's circle of friends is quite unlike the stolidly working-class society John comes from, where father is a patriarch and mother is maternal, where the

4. Introduction, *Jill*, p. 11.

front room is preserved for use only on special occasions, where father speaks a dialect.

The alternative is the society of the other working-class scholars in the college. The Christopher of this society is Whitbread. He is determined to 'get on': he works like a machine, in much the same way as John worked before Oxford. Whitbread, in John's mother's phrase, is 'of his own standing'; but he is also repulsive. Whenever we meet Whitbread, he is cramming food into his mouth, whether forking in whole potatoes, or scraping up custard with his spoon. He is physically ugly, mean, and always concerned to 'make an impression' on those who may be of use to him. In fact, Whitbread and Christopher are alike in being totally mercenary about their human contacts; Christopher is more attractive only in that his surface glitters more. John is sensitive enough to detest Whitbread, but gullible enough to be taken in by Christopher. Emulating Crouch, John's former English master, had got him to Oxford; copying Christopher, John thinks, will enable him to survive there.

John's going to Oxford destroys the continuity of his life, in disrupting the pattern established by his upbringing. This fact is emphasised in one of the most effective parts of the novel, when John hears that his home town has been blitzed. He travels home, having no news of whether his parents have survived the raid or not, and finds Huddlesford in ruins, an image of the 'waste land' he had felt would open before him at Oxford if he failed to win the friendship of Christopher. He is relieved to find his parents' house undamaged, and a note pinned to the door, saying they are in Preston, staying with a relative. John still has parents, but his scouting round the parental home, staring through the windows to see all more or less unchanged, symbolises just how far he is now excluded from his native place. There it is, perfect; but he can only stare in from a landscape that has lost all its landmarks. He is surrounded by wreckage, with—literally— only question marks looming above it here and there:

Dozens of places he knew well had been wrecked:
the local dingy cinema, fish shop; great gouts of clay
had been flung against posters. As he walked he looked
at the ruins, tracing the effects of single explosions

on groups of buildings, great tearing blows that left iron twisted into semi-interrogative shapes.[5]

But Christopher's society will not accept John, though he had thought he had secured his idol's friendship. John finds out the true state of Christopher's feelings towards him by accident. Christopher gets rid of his room-mate for an afternoon, wanting the place to himself in order to facilitate the carefully-planned seduction of his girl friend, Elizabeth. John leaves the rooms soon after Elizabeth's arrival, and as he shuts the door he overhears her comment on how well he has been 'trained', and Christopher's guffaws about the fact that they are drinking from John's china and eating his butter.

> He heard Elizabeth explode with laughter.
> 'Well, of all the —! It's too bad. He *must* be a feeble sort of worm.'
> 'Mother said he looked stuffed.'
> 'Stuffed! That's *just* the word!'[6]

Again, John is completely disorientated, realising that their openly expressed attitudes had been hypocritical. He no longer knows how to behave. Just as the patterns of behaviour he had established at home were inappropriate for Oxford, he sees now that his attitudes towards Christopher and his society will no longer do. Significantly, his new desolation is expressed in metaphors of wrecked masonry. The pattern established by his upbringing has been disrupted; his home town is to be literally ruined; his attempt to build a new edifice in Oxford is metaphorically ruined.

> How should he face Christopher now? And at this thought the last remnants of his illusion collapsed like the last wall of a demolished house. After all, then, he was on his own; he had failed, utterly and ignominiously failed to weave himself into the lives of these people.

5. *Jill*, p. 215
6. *Jill*, p. 111.

PHILIP LARKIN

>And as he had feared, the door had swung open again
>and he was alone again, doubly alone. The days would
>be scrappy, bits and pieces of action. No objects, no
>continuity.[7]

On the collapse of one illusion, John invents another.
Christopher seems to regret only one thing in his life, and that
is his tenuous family connections, especially his estrangement
from his sister. In order to strike back at Christopher, John
invents a younger sister, Jill, with whom he is supposed to have
a very close relationship. However, in his lack of 'objects' and
'continuity', 'Jill' becomes the only fixed point in his life, and the
fantasy soon takes over for its own sake. He writes to Jill, and
expresses to her his real feelings about Christopher and his friends
—although he writes in much the same way as those friends might
write to each other. The letters are a way of achieving Christopher's status, and by their means he is able to place himself—
writing establishes the continuity he misses by fixing him in a
relationship with another person.

In comparison with the life he invents for Jill, John sees how
colourless his own life is. Jill comes to the forefront of his consciousness:

>Suddenly it was she who was important, she who was
>interesting, she whom he longed to write about;
>beside her, he and his life seemed dusty and
>tedious.[8]

He finds that he is able to build up a much fuller and richer
image of Jill by erasing himself from the picture. He begins to
compile a continuous narrative about a young girl who has his
own sensibilities and sensitivity, but Christopher Warner's
advantages. She is of the middle classes, and attends 'Willow
Gables', a minor public school, an Angela Brazil version of
Christoper Warner's Lamprey. But like John, she is unhappy in
her social situation—her best friend leaves the school, and her
father dies. John had lost his father too, though in a different way.

7. *Jill*, p. 114.
8. *Jill*, p. 135.

40

Finding herself alone, she conceives a 'crush' on an older girl—much as John had had a 'crush' on Christopher. The great difference is that the older girl behaves towards Jill in the way that John would have had Christopher behave towards him. Having fleshed out Jill with a solid situation and background, he goes on to write a more or less daily diary for her.

John is really attempting the impossible: he wants a relationship with someone else, but as Jill is his creation, she can never be independent of him. But just as he concedes the impossibility of his task, he sees a young girl who fits almost exactly the description of his imaginary Jill. He devotes all his time to getting to meet her, and finally does, ironically enough through the agency of Christopher. The real Jill is Elizabeth's cousin.

Through Christopher John meets Jill formally, but when he tries to get to know her, he finds that she is not as eager for his friendship as he is for hers. John is delighted to find that 'Jill's' name is in fact almost that: Gillian. But when he calls her Jill, she insists that he use the full form of her name. In doing this, she symbolically refuses her part in John's fantasies, though he does not realise this at the time.

> 'It seemed I knew you—I knew your name was Jill—'
> 'It's not Jill!' During a lull in the traffic her voice
> rang out perhaps more sharply than she had intended,
> and she turned, for the first time a laugh broke over
> her face, drawing back her mouth, heightening her
> savage cheekbones. 'I'm sorry, that's just a thing with
> me. I told you yesterday—oh, no, you weren't there.
> No, I won't be called anything but Gillian,
> please . . .'[9]

At this point, their conversation is interrupted, and John arranges to see her for tea the following afternoon; but in the end, their meeting is prevented by Elizabeth.

Soon afterwards, Huddlesford is bombed. One after another, all his defences have crumbled—family, hopes of friendship with Christopher, the illusion of Jill, the Gillian whom he hoped might play 'Jill''s part. Now his inner state is externalised—the ruined

9. *Jill*, p. 192–3.

city is an analogue of his attempts to orientate himself. Returning to Oxford, he evaluates his life: the wrecked town has taught him something.

> And then again, it was like being told: see how little
> anything matters. All that anyone has is the life that
> keeps him going, and see how easily that can be patted
> out. See how appallingly little life is.[10]

John reorientates himself according to this lesson. It is not that he has found some landmarks, but that he has recognised that there are no landmarks, and seen the futility either of expecting others to provide them, or of inventing illusory ones. When he is next together with Christopher and his friends, he has lost the over-solicitousness that marked his behaviour before: he helps himself to beer, the nervous 'Er . . .' with which previously he had prefixed everything he said has disappeared, he refuses to lend Christopher money, and even asks his former idol to give him a cigarette. In fact, he has gained Christopher's assurance through his own new indifference. When he meets Elizabeth again, he reacts much as Christopher might:

> 'Good-bye,' he said, yawning. 'Bitch,' he added to
> himself, stirring his coffee.[11]

When he meets Jill for the last time, it is again as Christopher might. He has spent the evening drinking, alone, and finally he staggers to a party he knows her to be attending. As she leaves with Elizabeth and Christopher, John steps before her, takes her in his arms, and kisses her. Christopher knocks him down, and then, with the help of others, throws him into the college fountain. After his drenching, John contracts bronchial pneumonia. In his fevered state, he dreams out his relationship with Jill, and comes to the realisation that their fantasy relationship has worn thin—the love he bore her has died. Reflecting that this death seems inevitable whether the relationship is illusory or no, whether love is fulfilled or no, his conviction of 'how little anything matters' is reinforced:

10. *Jill*, p. 219.
11. *Jill*, p. 225.

Let him take this course, or this course, but still behind
the mind, on some other level, the way he had rejected
was being simultaneously worked out and the same
conclusion was being reached. What did it matter which
road he took if they both led to the same place?[12]

The trees outside his bedroom window are an appropriate image
of his view of life. Bent randomly here and there by a furious
wind over which they have no control, they none the less return
again and again to the vertical. John's conclusion is something
like the conclusion Larkin himself reaches in a mature poem,
'Dockery and Son' where he says of life:

Whether or not we use it, it goes,
And leaves what something hidden from us chose,[13]

John's outlook on life is bleak at the end of *Jill*; but at least he
has lost his passivity, at least made an autonomous gesture. The
book ends with John's parents coming to collect him, and
Christopher leaving the college with Elizabeth for the Christmas
vacations. As they say good-bye to the porter, a small white
dog sniffs his way from the street into the college. At first he
cowers as the porter threatens him; but he becomes bolder, and
when Elizabeth tries to coax him towards her he growls. The dog
has repeated John's gesture.

Jill is not so much about conflicting social situations, and the
stresses attendant on crossing class boundaries, as about our
reactions to life and our expectations of it. John is unable to cope
with life when he has no fixed context within which to live. He
demands continuity, and fixed objects by which to determine his
position. The question, 'How shall I behave?' is always answered
for John by reference to his place in a scheme. The lesson he
learns is that life's landscape really has no such fixed points,
no constant pattern. We cannot expect anything from life because
in the end we have no control over it, no more than the trees
have control over the way they bend.

12. *Jill*, p. 243.
13. *T.W.W.*, p. 38.

Larkin has commented that both his novels are really extended poems: he was careful, he said, if he used a word on page 15, not to use it again on page 115.[14] Certainly, we may criticise *Jill* for being too 'poetical'. Sometimes detail is so fine as to be pedantic, and not at all illuminating. It may flesh out John's background for us to know that his mother tied his sandwiches 'firmly, but not tightly';[15] but we are no better off for knowing that the apple eaten by the clergyman who shares John's railway carriage as he travels to Oxford is russet, nor that it is peeled with a *silver* pen-knife. In this first novel Larkin was too often lured into description for the sake of showing how well he can do it. Similarly, the young novelist is often carried away into drawing comparisons through similes that in no way advance the story or illuminate the theme. The events of the afternoon when he would have entertained Gillian to tea lay like a weight on John's mind, we are told; but when Whitbread informs him of the Huddlesford air-raid, the news makes the weight 'seem as flimsy as a paper decahedron'.[16] Such similes are striking, but, not being organic, stand out unnaturally from the narrative. In its dramatic over-statement of the hero's emotions, this incident suggests that the young novelist was labouring under the influence of Lawrence.

But if Larkin's description of particular objects is sometimes over-precise, it seems that his general presentation of war-time Oxford is less precise than it should be. The introduction to the second edition of *Jill* might be read as a comment on the accuracy of the novel itself. Though there are many of the real trappings of war-time—black-outs, rations, and so on—many of the events of the novel would not look out of place in *Decline and Fall*, where Evelyn Waugh describes some of the tricks played on Oxford undergraduates in the 'twenties. The getting drunk, being caught by proctors, throwing people in fountains, stapling others to college lawns with croquet hoops, all of which happen in *Jill*, accord ill with Larkin's claim that 'Life in college was austere. Its pre-war pattern had been dispersed, in some

14. Ian Hamilton, 'Four Conversations: Philip Larkin', *London Magazine*, IV, May 1964, p. 75.
15. *Jill*, p. 22.
16. *Jill*, p. 203.

instances permanently.'[17] They belong to an earlier, gayer decade. Similarly, Larkin reflects in his introduction that 'Traditional types such as aesthete and hearty were pruned relentlessly back.'[18] Christopher Warner is almost the caricature of the hearty.

It is unfortunate, too, that John's character is not consistent. Larkin wanted to present us with a naïve young man, quite out of things in the company of a group of young sophisticates—he does not understand that when 'Town' is referred to, the speaker is talking about London; he is baffled by the potions on Christopher's washstand ('What was "shaving lotion", and "talcum powder"?') and by his room-mate's slang. And yet when he becomes involved with the fantasy Jill, he has a perfect command of the idiom appropriate to a girls' boarding school.

These points are niggling, perhaps in view of the novel's many good qualities. It would have been worth writing the rest of the novel around its great *coup de théâtre* alone, when Jill, whom the reader has understood all along to be John's fantasy, appears in the flesh. Larkin's dialogue is excellent. He catches perfectly the accents and style of the young people on whom he bases his characters: the false emphases of the coquettish Elizabeth, the swagger of Christopher, the cynical wit of Patrick. Best of all, Larkin pinpoints the acutely self-conscious shyness of the immature young man who is thrust into an unfamiliar social setting, and makes John Kemp's retreat into fantasy perfectly convincing. Edmund Crispin, recalling the Larkin he knew at Oxford as a young man of about John Kemp's age, declares that the two have little in common: 'that massive, affable, pipe-smoking undergraduate was no Kemp.'[19] However, Larkin himself must have felt mortifications similar to Kemp's on occasions. In an interview with Ian Hamilton he said that as a youth he suffered from a bad stammer. 'Up to the age of 21,' he confessed, 'I was still asking for railway tickets by pushing written notes across the counter.'[20]

Many of the faults and extravagances of *Jill* are eradicated in

17. Introduction, *Jill*, p. 11.
18. *Jill*, p. 12.
19. 'An Oxford Group', p. 525.
20. 'Four Conversations', p. 76.

Larkin's second novel, *A Girl in Winter*. It was published in 1947, a particularly appropriate time, since the winter of 1946–7 had been the most severe of the century.

Like *Jill*, *A Girl in Winter* is a novel about maturing, coming to terms with the facts of our lives, accepting what is real, rather than depending on false expectations to make living worthwhile. John Kemp had been socially isolated, removed from his class by his education, and was not accepted by the new society he tried to move into at Oxford. Katherine Lind is more surely isolated than John was. She has lived in England for almost two years, a refugee from a continental country during war-time. We are not told her nationality; from her surname we can only guess that she does not come from a Latin country. This emphasises that the most important fact about her is not that she comes from such and such a background, being of such and such a race; but that she is alone, different, amongst a people who suspect her very foreignness. The town she lives in is provincial, but again, we know no more about it than that, for it is not named or geographically placed. Its sounds are deadened, its features obliterated by snow. (In fact, Larkin draws on some of the geographical features and place names of his home town, Coventry. But this knowledge must be brought to the book.) Even in her job of library assistant she holds no recognised position, being given only odd tasks to do. This 'stressed what was already sufficiently marked: that she was foreign and had no proper status there'.[21]

Despite her two years in England, Katherine knows no one, having made no friends, nor having sought any. Her isolation had depressed her, and when she first took refuge in England she had felt desolate at being severed from her background. Like John Kemp, she has adopted a strategy to make her life bearable: she clutches on to her past life through the objects she still has, which are associated with it. She is reluctant to buy new clothes, for to do so would be a symbolic acceptance of her present position:

> Nearly everything she possessed was a reference back to the days before she left home: her leather motoring-

21. *A.G.W.*, p. 25.

coat, for instance, was a relic of her student days . . .
Although she was not keen on mending, she spent many
evenings darning socks and underwear, with a sort
of love for them. They were all she had left.[22]

But even having recognised the falseness of her strategy, Katherine
cannot abandon her past completely. She clings tenaciously to
her memory of her one previous visit to England. She had started
up a school-organised pen-friendship with Robin Fennel, one of
two children in a middle class family which lived in a small
village near Oxford. At the age of sixteen, Katherine spent three
weeks with Robin and his sister, Jane, at their parents' home.
Her memory has not preserved a fully accurate record of her
English holiday: she is convinced that Robin had fallen in love
with her, and that the three weeks had been flawless. 'At once
whatever happened starts receding', as Larkin puts it in a poem
from *The Less Deceived*, and this is true for Katherine:

> those three nearly-forgotten weeks had taken on
> a new character in her memory. It was the only period
> of her life that had not been spoiled by later events,
> and she found that she could draw upon it
> hearteningly, remembering when she had been
> happy.[23]

The Fennels are the only people Katherine knows in England
but in the six years between her first visit and the outbreak of
war, the friendship had lapsed. On seeing a reference to Jane in
a newspaper, she had written again to the Fennels' old address.
Mrs Fennel had written back saying that she would let Robin
know Katherine's address. The anticipation of Robin's letter, and
more, the feeling that her renewed contact with the Fennels
might allow her to resign from her irksome job, has carried
Katherine through the couple of weeks before the action of the
novel begins. She can accept the barrenness of her life only if she
can regard it as temporary; and so she persuades herself that
the present is in parenthesis between the good time she had on

22. *A.G.W.*, p. 182.
23. *A.G.W.*, p. 185.

her previous visit to England, and the good time she is to have when her relationship with the Fennels is renewed.

But the very structure of the novel belies Katherine's attempts to romanticise her situation. The action takes place on a single winter Saturday; but the book is divided in three parts. The first deals with the events of the morning, during which she receives Robin Fennel's letter; the second with the first visit Katherine had paid to England; and the last with the afternoon and evening, when sentimentalised past and real present come into confrontation, with Robin Fennel's calling on her. Though Katherine's state of mind had persuaded her that the opposite is the case, it is the summer interlude, not the winter present, that is in parenthesis.

During the Saturday morning, Katherine had had a more accurate experience of the incidence of real happiness. She had been asked to help home Miss Green, a girl from the library who had been suffering from toothache. In helping the girl, Katherine suddenly achieves a sympathy with her such as she has not felt for as long as she can remember. The sensation of happiness is much like that sudden, unexpected one that is described in poem XXXII of *The North Ship*:

> for the first time in months she had happiness to spare, and now that her passive, pregnant expectation had suddenly found its outlet, it was all the more eager for having come so casually and unexpectedly.[24]

This is, perhaps, the state Katherine would hope to be more or less permanent on her being reunited with the Fennels.

Maturity, Katherine realises, means casting off the illusions she had cherished as a defence against an unpleasant life; but though she is intellectually able to understand the necessity of shedding misconceptions about the past and the possibility of the past being repeated, her emotions will not yet allow her to see her present life except as an interlude before the resumption of the idyll she still imagines her English holiday to have been. Such a state of maturity is described as it was in *Jill*, in terms of crumbling buildings and a waste landscape:

24. *A.G.W.*, p. 35.

But once the break [with the past] was made, as though
continually-trickling sand had caused a building to slip
suddenly on its foundations so that perhaps one single
ornament fell to the floor, life ceased to be a confused
stumbling from one illumination to another, a series
of unconnected clearings in a tropical forest, and
became a flat landscape, wry and rather small, with
a few unforgettable landmarks somewhat resembling
a stretch of fen-land, where an occasional dyke or
broken fence shows up for miles, and the sails
of a mill turn all day long in the steady wind.[25]

Katherine must accept her life as having no real progression;
rather, it is a series of more or less arbitrary journeys forced upon
her. We often see Katherine making bus journeys in the course
of the novel—and we often see Larkin himself making similar
journeys, though usually by rail, in *The Less Deceived* and *The
Whitsun Weddings*. Katherine's bus journey to the home of Miss
Veronica Parbury, to return a handbag she had picked up by
mistake, is an analogue of her life. It is this chance meeting which
forces on her the truth about the Fennels and her relationship
with them. Through Miss Parbury, she glimpses 'the undertow
of peoples' relations, two-thirds of which is without face, with
only begging and lonely hands'.[26] On returning to the library,
Katherine finds that Miss Green has returned to work. They
meet again, and Katherine sees that the contact they had made
with each other that morning had been only temporary. Robin
will not lead her back to an idealised life, she realises: the contact
she had achieved with him was temporary, too. Her illusion was
'a pretty thought', she thinks: 'What a pretty thought it was, and
how untrue. She had known it was untrue . . . she had seized the
slightest chance of escaping the desolation that was pressing upon
her.'[27]

When Katherine meets Robin Fennel again, it seems that he
too has made similar perceptions about his life. As a young man,
he had been chiefly remarkable for his quiet certainty about his

25. *A.G.W.*, p. 183.
26. *A.G.W.*, pp. 199–200.
27. *A.G.W.*, p. 217.

future. The sixteen-year-old Katherine was frustrated by a sense of 'barren perfection' that seemed to surround him, by his 'almost supernatural maturity'.[28] In the light of what Katherine later comes to realise, maturity does not consist in such certainty. Robin's scheme of things is shaken by the war. When Katherine asks him whether he still intends to go into the Foreign Office, he replies that 'everything's so uncertain'.[29] He has made no plans for when the war is over: 'After the war doesn't exist for me. I just look forward about a week.'[30] Robin has reached the stage at which Katherine had found herself soon after her return to England. For Robin, war has just 'made a mess of things':

> "Broken the sequence, so to speak. I mean, I knew
> pretty well what I was going to do, my career and so
> forth. All gone to blazes.'[31]

We may remember that what so desolated John Kemp was the conviction that in his life, in his loneliness, there would be 'no continuity'.

When Robin asks if he may sleep with her, Katherine points out that it will not mean anything; but she does not refuse. Earlier in the day, she thought she had reached and comforted Miss Green, but even then, faced with the other's pain and suffering, Katherine had felt powerless. Everyone is isolated from everyone else, in the end. Acknowledging the poverty of personal relationships was one of the recognitions she had to make in breaking with the past. If sleeping with Robin will mean nothing, there is no reason why she should do so—but then, there is also no reason why she should not. As John Kemp had reflected, 'What does it matter which road he took if they both led to the same place?'

But this acceptance is not merely negative. There is a kind of affirmation in the acceptance itself, in Katherine's recognition that life had 'shrunken slightly into the truth'.[32] Larkin was

28. *A.G.W.*, p. 109.
29. *A.G.W.*, p. 239.
30. *A.G.W.*, p. 240.
31. *A.G.W.*, p. 246.
32. *A.G.W.*, p. 217.

surely thinking of Yeats here, for the observation is strongly
reminiscent of the last line of 'The Coming of Wisdom With
Time':

> Through all the lying days of my youth
> I swayed my leaves and flowers in the sun;
> Now I may wither into the truth.[33]

In writing of 'the truth' Yeats withered only in the sense that his
poetry became less fey. Truth is not necessarily beauty, as Yeats
implies, but he certainly made great poetry from it, whereas he
had only made good minor poetry from his 'leaves and flowers'.
Similarly, from an affirmation of bleakness, Larkin makes one
of the most memorable pieces of prose in *A Girl in Winter*.
Katherine's and Robin's dreams

> were going in orderly slow procession, moving from
> darkness further into darkness, allowing no suggestion
> that their order should be broken, or that one day,
> however many years distant, the darkness would begin
> to give place to light.
> Yet their passage was not saddening. Unsatisfied
> dreams rose and fell about them, crying out against
> their implacability, but in the end glad that such order,
> such destiny, existed. Against this knowledge, the
> heart, the will, and all that made for protest, could
> at last sleep.[34]

A Girl in Winter is a better novel than *Jill*, largely because of
the stylistic improvements on the earlier work. As a story, it is
slighter—much more an 'over-sized poem', which Larkin now
considers both novels to be. But the prose, in the main, is much
sparer. There is still the occasional redundant simile, as when
Katherine's vacillating emotions are compared at length to a
flock of birds swooping first to one corner of a field and then to
another. Really, for a state already fully described, we do not
need to be given an explanatory image that adds nothing new.
There is much less self-conscious 'fine writing' than in *Jill*;

33. *Collected Poems*, p. 105.
34. *A.G.W.*, p. 248.

though the young novelist was so impressed with one figure from his first novel that he repeats it in his second: the protagonist's face is covered with fine rain (in *Jill*) or cold air (in *A Girl in Winter*), like 'wet muslin'.

Larkin has a firmer grasp of the complexities of character in *A Girl in Winter*. The portrait of Anstey (a rough anagram of 'nasty', perhaps), the acting librarian where Katherine works, has vicious satirical bite. Anstey is ostentatiously self-educated pompous and conceited; determined, now that the war has forced advancement his way, to be as much of a petty tyrant as he can, particularly over those whose natural advantages exceed his own. He uses his position to insult Katherine, and his tirade against the girl for some trivial mistake, a superb piece of satirical observation and tangible expression of character, shows exactly how mean the man is. Katherine's hatred of Anstey is quite justified. But, quite by accident, she learns how his personal and emotional life is being ruined by the senile but cunning and unscrupulous invalid mother of the woman he wishes to marry, who capitalises on her daughter's feelings of filial duty to frustrate the marriage. The woman is Miss Veronica Parbury, who had unburdened herself to Katherine, a stranger to her previously, during their chance meeting. Knowledge of 'the undertow of people's relations', seen in the emotional life of Anstey and Miss Parbury, is perhaps what informs Katherine's decision to let Robin stay. Even a man as despicable as Anstey deserves compassion, and when Katherine flings her knowledge in his face, having been provoked by another insult, she regrets it, while trying to excuse herself with the thought that he asked for it.

Despite Edmund Crispin's warning, that we should not look in *Jill* for 'portents of the notable poet-to-come',[35] the novels are interesting for those who wish to come to a fuller knowledge of Larkin's verse, as well as for those who like reading good novels. It is true that *Jill* holds less interest with regard to Larkin's poetry than *A Girl in Winter*; though in the earlier novel we do meet, tangentially, a character whose name is familiar, even to those who know only Larkin's anthology-pieces. John Kemp's teacher, Crouch, reprimanding his class, picks on one 'Bleaney' in particular. Perhaps this is the Bleaney of Larkin's well-known

35. 'An Oxford Group', p. 525.

'Mr Bleaney', finding life pushing him about even at school age. But the novels, like *The North Ship*, explore some of the themes to which Larkin will return in his later poetry. Both books deal with the way we 'pick up bad habits of expectancy', as Larkin puts it in 'Next Please'. We build illusions—and 'build' is an important word here, for both books express the tendency by metaphors of construction and demolition—to interrupt what Katherine Lind finally realises is a more barren and flat landscape than we pretend. Both deal with the distance between people, even those who would like to be closest to one another: Larkin was later to write poems on this topic. And a theme expressed in *The North Ship* has an important place in *A Girl in Winter*, at least: our powerlessness before the passage of time. Robin cannot bear the ticking of Katherine's watch: it keeps him awake, and reminds him, perhaps, that the time he spends with Katherine is no more than an interlude. Larkin's poetry returns so often to this topic that Anthony Thwaite has said that 'The Music of Time' might be an appropriate title for his work as a whole.[36]

'A very crude difference between novels and poetry,' Larkin has suggested, explaining why he stopped writing fiction, 'is that novels are about other people and poetry is about yourself.'[37] Perhaps writing *Jill* and *A Girl in Winter* forced his work to take on qualities he later attributed to photography, an art that 'will not censor blemishes', and

> overwhelmingly persuades
> That this is a real girl in a real place,
> In every sense empirically true![38]

This is certainly what was needed in order to eradicate the faults of *The North Ship* from his later poetry; and if writing the novels did not cause the new orientation of *XX Poems* and *The Less Deceived*, it was at least a good exercise in creating real people in real places.

36. 'The Poetry of Philip Larkin', p. 46.
37. Ian Hamilton, 'Four Conversations', p. 75.
38. 'Lines On A Young Lady's Photograph Album', *T.L.D.*, p. 13.

4   *The Less Deceived*

Of the twenty-nine poems in *The Less Deceived*, thirteen had previously appeared in the 1951 *XX Poems*. 'Deceptions', from which the title of the book was taken, appeared in the pamphlet, as well as 'Wedding Wind', 'At Grass', 'Latest Face', 'If, My Darling' and 'Wants'. 'Church Going', one of the most famous as well as one of the best poems of the 'fifties, was not written until 1954; but none the less, the list of poems that appeared in both *XX Poems* and *The Less Deceived* shows that in 1951 Larkin was already the poet he showed himself to be in 1955, and quite different from the one who wrote *The North Ship*.

That in his first book Larkin followed the example of Yeats so closely, writing of experiences that would not look out of place in Yeats's work, as well as using his tone of voice, his stylistic tricks and his versification, indicates that the young poet was more concerned to write poetry than to express his ideas and feelings through verse. He stated his own problem in poem XVII:

> To write one song, I said,
> As sad as the sad wind
> That walks around my bed,
> Having one simple fall
> As a candle-flame swells, and is thinned,
> As a curtain stirs by the wall
> —For this I must visit the dead.[1]

That is, he has no confidence that the world around him can provide him with substance for his poetry; he must turn either to an admired and great poet and borrow his metaphors and tones, or to a stock of standard romanticisms. It may be that moving away from Oxford and university society, gaining experience of people quite different from himself, and being

1. *T.N.S.*, p. 29.

forced to look critically at others and at his surroundings for the purposes of novel writing made the young writer less inward looking. This may just have come from growing older. He has not offered any such explanation for the change we see in *XX Poems*; but he has suggested that reading Hardy's poetry, with which he was unacquainted till the age of twenty-five, did make a profound difference: not until then did he really see that the borrowing and sentimentality that mars *The North Ship* is fustian, and that poetry may be made from simple, personal human emotions and everyday events.

Writing to an American student, Larkin said that after *The North Ship*, 'I looked to Hardy rather than to Yeats as my ideal, and eventually a more rational approach, less hysterical and emphatic, asserted itself.'[2] He dates his reaction against Yeats fairly exactly in his introduction to the 1966 edition of his first book: 'In early 1946 I had some new digs in which the bedroom faced east, so that the sun woke me inconveniently early. I used to read. One book I had at my bedside was the little blue *Chosen Poems of Thomas Hardy*: Hardy I knew as a novelist, but as regards his verse I shared Lytton Strachey's verdict that "the gloom is not even relieved by a little elegance of diction". This opinion did not last long; if I were asked to date its disappearance, I should guess it was the morning I first read "Thoughts of Phena at News of her Death".'[3] Hardy seems to have assisted a change in Larkin rather than prompted it. Speaking in a radio broadcast later transcribed and published in the *Listener* in 1968, Larkin said that Hardy was not a young man's poet; when he began to read Hardy himself, he realised that 'here was somebody writing about things I was beginning to feel myself'.[4]

Hardy's influence on Larkin was not of the same nature as Yeats's. Yeats had given the young poet a verbal model, a distinctive tone of voice to imitate. Hardy's influence was less direct. I have already said that the theme of poem *XXXII*, the poem added to *The North Ship* in its second edition to show 'the

2. Judith Anne Johnson, 'The Development of Philip Larkin's Poetry', unpublished M.A. dissertation, North Dakota State University 1965, pp. 29–30.
3. *T.N.S.*, p. 10.
4. 'Philip Larkin Praises the Poetry of Thomas Hardy', *Listener*, 25 July 1968, p. 111.

Celtic fever abated', is a theme that is characteristically Hardy's—the feeling that we only fully appreciate our affection for someone when we have lost her, or him. But this is not an imitation of one of Hardy's themes in the same sense that poem *XX*, 'I see a girl dragged by the wrists', the poem about poetic creation being bought at the expense of worldly and sensual gratifications, is an imitation of the Yeatsian theme of 'Perfection of the life, or of the work.' The abstractness of poem *XX*, and the fact that such characters and incidents as there are might have been culled from Yeats's *Collected Poems*, persuades me that the topic is not felt as immediately and personally as that of poem *XXXII*. Larkin does not imitate Hardy; he learns from him.

It is true that there is the odd borrowing from Hardy in Larkin's work: I mentioned Larkin's unusual use of the word 'prinked' in 'Next Please', which is used in the same way in Hardy's superb 'Beeny Cliff'. Reading Hardy, one sometimes feels, 'Larkin might almost have written that'. These lines from 'He Abjures Love' are an example:

> But—after love what comes?
> A scene that lours,
> A few sad vacant hours,
> And then, the Curtain.[5]

And occasionally, as in the final lines of 'Dockery and Son', one feels that Larkin sounds like Hardy. But we never feel, 'Hardy *did* write that!'—though I think someone might be excused for believing Yeats to be the author of 'Damn all explanatory rhymes', or 'a sack of meal upon two sticks', or

> What beasts now hesitate
> Clothed in cloudless air,
> In whom desire stands straight?[6]

But the nature of Hardy's influence in the verse Larkin wrote after *The North Ship* may best be seen by reference to the poem from which *The Less Deceived* draws its title.

5. Thomas Hardy, *Collected Poems*, 4th edition, London 1968, p. 221.
6. *T.N.S.*, p. 11.

At first sight, though, 'Deceptions' might remind us of Betjeman rather than Hardy. It takes its starting point from a piece of Victorian prose of anthropological interest, much as Betjeman makes his balladic 'Sir John Piers' from the story of that 'bold bad baronet' in James Woods's *Annals of Westmeath Ancient and Modern*, or, more appositely, 'An Incident in the Early Life of Ebenezer Jones, Poet, in 1828', from an introduction to Jones's *Studies of Sensation and Event*, written by his brother. Betjeman reprints the prose source of his poem, and Larkin reprints the short passage from Mayhew's *London Labour and the London Poor* that is the starting point of 'Deceptions'. Both 'Ebenezer Jones' and 'Deceptions' are about the despoiling of an innocent, and are set in nineteenth-century London. Larkin's description is impressionistic, where Betjeman's is literal, but it gives us quite as convincing a feel of the London of a different age:

> The sun's occasional print, the brisk brief
> Worry of wheels along the street outside
> Where bridal London bows the other way,[7]

The alliterated 'w' creates the rush of the carriage wheels, all ignoring the raped girl who is the subject of the poem; the repeated 'b' suggests the sound of the bells booming ironically across London for a wedding.

But even in relation to this starting point, we can see connections with Hardy; and, as in the case of poem XXXII from *The North Ship*, particularly with the Hardy that appears in those poems marking the height of his achievement, the remorseful *Poems of 1912–13*. In 'Deceptions' Larkin is not implicated in the woman's tragedy in the way that Hardy was in his wife's. In her later years, Emma Lavinia was less than sane, and had delusions of grandeur, considering that she had married beneath her, being related to an archdeacon, even though Hardy was at the time one of the most distinguished living men of letters. Hardy would have been less than human if he had not felt that he hated her at times, or forgotten that this was a woman whom he had loved profoundly. Larkin is implicated in the raped girl's tragedy only in so far as he sympathises with her predicament;

7. *T.L.D.*, p. 37.

but he speaks directly to the wronged woman, back through the years, much as Hardy addresses Emma Lavinia. They have a similar mood: regretful, consoling, yet aware of the futility of consolation. We might compare particularly three lines from the second stanza of 'Deceptions' with three from Hardy's 'After a Journey'.

> What can be said,
> Except that suffering is exact, but where
> Desire takes charge, readings will grow erratic?
> > ('Deceptions')
> What have you now found to say of our past—
> Scanned across the dark space wherein I have lacked
> > you?
> Summer gave us sweets, but autumn wrought division?
> > ('After a Journey')

'Hardy taught one to feel rather than to write,'[8] Larkin once said, and here there is more similarity of emotion and attitude than verbal echo, for Larkin's language is contemporary, and very much his own.

Further, the theme of 'Deceptions' is a theme central both to Larkin's and to Hardy's work. When *The Less Deceived* was published, its title was seen, understandably, as connoting a certain stance towards experience, an unwillingness to be taken in, a warning that the author was no one's fool. It was rather like the titles of volumes by other Movement poets: John Wain had published *Mixed Feelings*, Kingsley Amis *A Frame of Mind*, Elizabeth Jennings *A Way of Seeing*, Donald Davie *The Brides of Reason*. But this is to obscure the real significance of 'Deceptions': it is not about being careful not to be duped, but about suffering, and its maturing effects. Larkin himself has emphasised the centrality of this theme in Hardy's work. Reviewing a critical volume on Hardy, he asks, 'What is the intensely maturing experience of which Hardy's modern man is most sensible? In my view it is suffering, or sadness.'[9] Larkin insists that this is not

8. 'Philip Larkin Praises the Poetry of Thomas Hardy', p. 111.

9. Philip Larkin, 'Wanted: Good Hardy Critic', *Critical Quarterly*, VIII (Summer 1966), p. 177.

a negative attitude towards experience, a warning that we should avoid life, that only in that way will we avoid suffering. Hardy's work, he says, is a 'continual imaginative celebration of what is both the truest and the most important element in life, most important in the sense of most necessary to spiritual development'.[10] This is surely just what Larkin is saying in 'Deceptions': the only consolation he can offer the girl is that her suffering is 'exact'. She will spiritually grow and mature by her knowledge; the 'fulfilment' of the rapist is in reality not fulfilling, but disappointing, a blundering into empty confusion. In her knowledge, the girl, like Katherine Lind, can at least be 'glad that such order, such destiny, existed'.

'When I came to Hardy,' Larkin has said, 'it was with the sense of relief that I didn't have to try and jack myself up to a concept of poetry that lay outside my own life—this is perhaps what I felt Yeats was trying to make me do.'[11] Hardy is 'not a transcendental writer,' Larkin went on, 'he's not a Yeats, he's not an Eliot; his subjects are men, the life of men, time and the passing of time, love and the fading of love.'[12] The list applies equally to Larkin's own verse. Hardy taught Larkin to draw on what he actually saw and felt strongly about for his work, rather than on what he ideally saw, or what he believed he ought to feel strongly about. The young poet no longer worried that the real events, objects, emotions and feelings of his own life were not fit material for poetry.

Larkin's critical writings, mainly in the form of reviews of poets he likes, have outlined the concept of poetry Hardy gave him—a set of beliefs that have remained remarkably constant over the years. The most important of those beliefs is that a poem should directly depend on actual experience. He has said that 'the impulse to preserve lies at the bottom of all art',[13] and describes one of his poems as an attempt to 'pickle'[14] an experience in verse. In a short preface to a selection of his poems in D. J. Enright's *Poets of the 1950's*, Larkin explained: 'I write

10. 'Wanted: Good Hardy Critic', p. 178.
11. 'Philip Larkin Praises the Poetry of Thomas Hardy', p. 111.
12. *Ibid.*
13. *Poets of the 1950's*, p. 77.
14. 'Speaking of Writing XIII: Philip Larkin', p. 16.

PHILIP LARKIN

poems to preserve things I have seen/thought/felt (if I may so indicate a composite and complex experience) both for myself and for others, though I feel that my prime responsibility is to the experience itself.'[15]

Moreover, these experiences should be 'unsorted'.[16] One of the chief defects of modern and contemporary poetry, Larkin believes, is that poetry is losing touch with life because the experiences that inform it are too often of a rarefied kind. Reviewing Auden's *Homage to Clio* Larkin suggests that in his later verse, Auden 'took a header into literature'; and he regrets that since the Second World War, Auden no longer shows his 'deep abhorrence',

> If I caught anyone preferring Art
> To Life and Love and being Pure-in-Heart.[17]

This explains one of Larkin's most widely quoted, and most widely misunderstood remarks. Later in the *Poets of the 1950's* anthology, he indicates briefly what he considers to be wrong with contemporary poetry. (It is worth noting, incidentally, that when Larkin wrote this preface, he was not aware that Enright was going to print it. As far as he was concerned, he was writing a personal letter to an editor who was going to print some of his poems, not a formal introduction to his work.) 'I . . . have no belief in "tradition",' Larkin wrote, 'or a common myth-kitty or casual allusions in poems to other poems or poets, which last I find unpleasantly like the talk of literary understrappers letting you see they know the right people.'[18] The statement has been taken again and again by those who dislike Larkin's poetry as evidence of a 'provincial', even philistine frame of mind. The charge has no substance if we appreciate fully what Larkin is saying: he is objecting to '"tradition"' (the quotation marks are important), the 'myth-kitty' and those 'casual allusions' in so far

15. *Poets of the 1950's*, p. 77.
16. Larkin used the phrase 'unsorted experience' in introducing 'Faith Healing', on the Marvell Press recording, 'Philip Larkin Reads and Comments on *The Whitsun Weddings*', Listen Records (LPV 6), 1965.
17. Philip Larkin, 'What's Become of Wystan?', *Spectator*, 15 July 1960, p. 104.
18. *Poets of the 1950's*, p. 78.

as they are considered separate from other experience. Of course, reading a poem or knowing a poet is as much a part of experience as what happens at work, or watching two horses grazing; but that is the point: poems and poets are not things apart. He objects to '"tradition"' considered as something above and beyond life; to a 'myth-kitty', a stock of special 'poetic' myths which are to poetry as stage properties are to drama; to 'casual allusions', which are not organic to the poem, and are not really casual at all, but a way of showing off. Poetry should have a direct relationship with life, then, in that it should be regarded as being a part of life, not separate from it, and it should look to life for its subject matter.

More than this, Larkin has consistently maintained that a poet should write about those things in life that move him most deeply: if he does not feel deeply about anything, he should not write. This explains his small poetic production, and his conviction that a poet should not make his living by writing. He believes that poetry will only be written well when it has to be written: 'one should . . . write poetry only when one wants to and has to',[19] he said to a *Times* correspondent in 1964, and more recently, in a radio broadcast to mark his fiftieth birthday, he insisted that 'writing isn't an act of the will'. Only when the poem has to be written will the 'poetic pressure',[20] as he calls it in his review of *Homage to Clio*, be high. The trouble with Auden's post-war poetry, he has said, is that it lacks this pressure; it is 'a poetry written it seems by someone no longer capable of strong feeling, or of conveying strong feeling in poetry'.[21] It is significant that Larkin attributes this lack of 'pressure' to Auden's having removed himself from the conditions that nourished his early poetry by moving to America. The life of pre-1939 Europe, that is, vitalised and provided the subject matter for Auden's best work. He has suggested that even Yeats, whose life was far fuller of obvious incident than Auden's, seems occasionally to be casting round for a subject about which to write poems. Again, in such cases, there is no 'pressure', no impression that the poet felt strongly about his subject matter. None of this is new, of

19. 'Speaking of Writing XIII: Philip Larkin', p. 16.
20. 'What's Become of Wystan?', p. 104.
21. Philip Larkin, 'No More Fever', *Listen*, II (Summer 1956), p. 24.

PHILIP LARKIN

course: the maxim that if the poet wishes to make us cry, he must
first have cried himself, is at least as old as Horace.

Larkin has praised Sir John Betjeman for writing poetry that
is not marred by this defect. Betjeman's poems obviously spring
from feelings of real importance to him, Larkin believes: they are
'exclusively about things that impress, amuse, excite, anger or
attract him, and—and this is most important—once a subject
has established its claim on his attention, he never questions the
legitimacy of his interest'.[22] It is surprising, perhaps, to consider
that Larkin's suggestions are in the same spirit as Wordsworth's,
that 'poetry is the spontaneous overflow of powerful feelings'.
Surprising, in view of the fact that Larkin has been singled out
as a poet who has little emotional intensity in his verse. M. L.
Rosenthal stated that the strongest emotion evident in Larkin's
poetry is self-pity; Jon Silkin, reviewing *The Whitsun Weddings*,
applauded Larkin's skill but deplored the lack of 'passion'.
Larkin himself is puzzled by critics' finding his work unemotional:
'I always think that the poems I write are very much more naïve
—very much more emotional—almost embarrassingly so—than a
lot of other people's. When I was tagged as unemotional, it
used to mystify me; I used to find it quite shaming to read some
of the things I'd written.'[23]

The feeling of responsibility to the experience justifies Larkin's
conviction that content in poetry is more important than form.
In the dust-jacket 'blurb' of the American edition of *The Whitsun
Weddings* he stated this belief very strongly: 'Form holds little
interest for me. Content is everything.' The statement is not
fully borne out by his poetic practice, as I shall show. The rhyme
schemes of 'I Remember, I Remember' and the recent 'The
Building' are extremely complex, and must have been worked
out through what Yeats calls 'the fascination of what's difficult';
and Anthony Thwaite has reported that Larkin told him he would
like to write a poem in which the stanzas were so complicated
that one could wander about in them as in the aisles and side-
chapels of a cathedral.

Larkin has not the contempt of form expressed by Emerson in
'Merlin':

22. Philip Larkin, 'Betjeman en Bloc', *Listen*, III (Spring 1959), p. 15.
23. Ian Hamilton, 'Four Conversations', pp. 74–5

> He shall not his brain encumber
> With the coils of rhythm and number.

It is just that originality, for Larkin, consists not in modifying the medium of communication, but in communicating something different. His favourite poets, he has said, in a more balanced statement than the one from the 'blurb' I quote above, are 'on the whole, people to whom technique seems to matter less than content, people who accept the forms they have inherited but use them to express their own content'.[24] At various times, he has pecifically named Christina Rossetti, William Barnes, Praed, Frost, Wilfred Owen, Auden (at least, the Auden who was writing before 1939), Betjeman, and above all, of course, Hardy.

But though Larkin considers his prime responsibility to be to the experience he is trying to preserve, he has a keen sense of the audience for his poems. 'If there is no . . . successful reading,' he has said, 'the poem can hardly be said to exist in a practical sense at all.'[25] It is partly the reverence for form over content that has made poetry a study rather than a pleasure, he believes: he deplores unnecessary obscurity in poetry, considering that poetry should be able to compete with television or radio. A correspondent for the *Times Educational Supplement*, in a short article on Larkin published in 1956, enraged certain critics when he claimed that 'With Larkin, poetry is on its way back to the middle-brow public.'[26] Charles Tomlinson took this up in a piece he entitled 'The Middle-brow Muse', and condemned Larkin for doing what he called 'the average man business in verse'.[27] In a later essay on contemporary poetry for the *Pelican Guide to English Literature*, Tomlinson sneers at Larkin's words as they are reported in the *Times Educational Supplement* article. For Larkin, Tomlinson says, 'the aim of poetry is . . . simply to "keep the child from its

24. Ian Hamilton, 'Four Conversations', p. 71.
25. Philip Larkin, 'The Pleasure Principle', *Listen*, II (Summer–Autumn 1957), p. 28.
26. 'Four Young Poets—I: Philip Larkin', p. 933.
27. Charles Tomlinson, 'The Middlebrow Muse', *Essays in Criticism*, VII (January 1957), p. 209.

television set and the old man from his pub".'[28] The key word here is 'simply'. Larkin did not claim that poetry was 'simply' anything: what he did claim in his rather joky corruption of Sidney is that poetry should at least give straightforward pleasure. 'The Pleasure Principle', as he has called it, is a necessary element in poetry; but he has never said that it is the only element.

It is true that Larkin seeks the general audience. He has commended Kipling, Housman and Betjeman for their 'direct relation with a reading public', obtained by being 'moving and memorable'.[29] 'If a poet loses his pleasure-seeking audience,' he insists, 'he has lost the only audience worth having, for which the dutiful mob that signs on every September is no substitute.'[30] Flatly stated, this does seem to lend support to those of his critics, like Charles Tomlinson and A. Alvarez, who claim that Larkin is not a 'serious' poet. 'He has never thrown his hat into the heavyweight ring,'[31] Alvarez has complained. The suggestion seems further justified by Larkin's frequent diatribes of the 'dutiful mob' variety, which find their way into his poetry—he complains in 'Vers de Société' of 'talking to that ass about his fool research',[32] and in 'Posterity' he draws a slashingly satirical portrait of 'Jake Balokowsky, my biographer'[33]—and perhaps more by his often stated belief that 'modernism', its central principle enshrined in Eliot's famous comment, 'Poets in our civilisation, as it exists at present, must be difficult,' has done more to corrupt the arts than to advance them. In the introduction to his volume of jazz criticism, *All What Jazz?*, he deplores the obscurity of the moderns, taking as their representatives Pound in poetry, Picasso in painting, and in jazz Charlie Parker, the saxophonist who did most to engineer the divergence of jazz into 'modern' and 'traditional'. Larkin considers ours 'an

28. Charles Tomlinson, 'Poetry Today', in *The Pelican Guide to English Literature: 7. The Modern Age*, ed. Boris Ford, 2nd edition, Harmondsworth 1964, p. 458.

29. Philip Larkin, 'The Blending of Betjeman', *Spectator*, 2 December 1960, p. 913.

30. 'The Pleasure Principle', p. 29.

31. A. Alvarez, 'Philip Larkin', in *Beyond All This Fiddle*, London, 1968, p. 85.

32. Philip Larkin, 'Vers de Société', *New Statesman*, 18 June 1971, p. 854.

33. Philip Larkin, 'Posterity', *New Statesman*, 28 June 1968, p. 876.

age so determined to make hard work out of reading poetry',[34] and complains that this is to a large extent the fault of critics: 'modern criticism thrives on the difficult—either on explaining the difficult or explaining that what seemed straightforward is in fact difficult.'[35] The reason why Betjeman's verse has received little attention from critics, he has said, is only that there is no exegesis to perform. Larkin is very much 'Against Interpretation', in Susan Sontag's phrase, and considers it nonsense for a critic to claim to know a poem's meaning more accurately than its author.

I should have more trepidation about writing this book if I thought that Larkin truly held the views he is often credited—or rather, damned—with, the anti-intellectual, anti-'serious', anti-critic views. This has been suggested as recently as 1972: in another article for the *Times Educational Supplement*, a correspondent refers to Larkin's 'mildly "anti-intellectual" outlook', and claims that at Oxford Larkin's sympathies were 'with the hearties'. As for this last, we have Larkin's own word, in the introduction to the second edition of *Jill*, if not in the text, that the labels 'hearty' and 'aesthete' did not really apply in the war years. And we have the incisive picture of a 'hearty' in Chrisopher Warner to compare the poet with. The statement that Larkin is '"anti-intellectual"'—in inverted commas or not—is surely a travesty. Would an 'anti-intellectual', on being asked what it felt like to be fifty in a recent radio broadcast, muse that it is 'rather sobering to realise one has lived longer than Arnold of Rugby, or Porson, the eighteenth-century professor of Greek'? Larkin is certainly anti- intellectual pretension, anti- that kind of cleverness designed not to enlighten but to confuse and exclude; but not anti- the intellectual in itself.

The opinion that modern criticism often seems to be concerned to explain 'that what seemed straightforward is in fact difficult', does not indicate that Larkin is opposed to the difficult, in itself. His attitude is clarified by a comment he made when reviewing John Press's study of obscurity in poetry, *The Chequer'd Shade*. Press had neglected to explain an important phenomenon, Larkin

34. Philip Larkin, 'The Poetry of William Barnes', *Listener*, 16 August 1962, p. 257.
35. 'Wanted: Good Hardy Critic', p. 174.

said: why it was, that 'forty or fifty years ago obscurity suddenly became fun in a way it never had been before'.[36] Obscurity that is 'fun' essentially has little to do with the poem itself. The poetic innovators of the first decades of this century, Larkin is saying, deliberately used obscurity as a barrier or a booby trap. Eliot did not call himself 'Old Possum' for nothing: who can read his notes to 'The Waste Land'—soberly directing us to a passage from Ovid, reproduced in the original Latin, which he declares to be of 'great anthropological interest'; or to a passage from Chapman's *Handbook of Birds of Eastern North America*, where the habitat and quality of song of the hermit thrush (*Turdus aonalaschkae pallasii*—of course) are described—without feeling that he is being gently twitted? E. M. Forster suggested that their function was actually to put readers off: he declared that the notes are deliberately misleading, and intended for those already confused, 'whom they will lead deeper into confusion'.[37]

But Larkin has never condemned Yeats for his difficulty, though Yeats is at times a difficult poet. So is Larkin himself, one might add. One of his closest friends and admirers, Kingsley Amis, recently objected that 'in one poem out of three, there's what I would call a wilfully eccentric word'.[38] For American readers, at least, there is an occasional reference to a peculiarly English ceremony that is baffling. One American postgraduate student quite misread Larkin's 'Broadcast'. She understood these lines which describe the rituals before the beginning of a concert, to express Larkin's anti-monarchist views:

> a sudden scuttle on the drum,
> 'The Queen', and huge resettling. Then begins
> A snivel on the violins:

The drums and snivelling violins, she thought, heralded the entrance of the Queen in person. Thus, Larkin despises the servility of the British under the tyrannical sway of Elizabeth II.

36. Philip Larkin, 'No Fun Any more', *Manchester Guardian*, 18 November 1958, p. 4.
37. E. M. Forster, 'T. S. Eliot', *Abinger Harvest*, Harmondsworth 1967, p. 105.
38. Kingsley Amis, in the Radio 3 Broadcast, 'Larkin at 50', 9 August 1972.

Of course, 'The Queen' is merely the shortened form of 'God Save the Queen', and the reference to 'snivelling' is a reference to the usual tuning-up before a concert, rather than a slight on the political complaisance of the British. Larkin is a monarchist, in fact, and not the reverse. The Irish sixpence the speaker drops into the collection box in 'Church Going' has occasioned some misunderstanding. It is suggested that the coin has absolutely no value for the speaker, and its contribution is a way of cocking a snook at the Church, and at religion. But if we happen to know that the poem was written in Ireland, and that Larkin lived there for four years, we can see that this is not necessarily so.

Larkin is perhaps culpable in these instances, but in general, his own practice shows us that it is unjustifiable difficulty he objects to. His distinction between what is unnecessarily obscure and what is properly hard to understand because the complexity of the subject demands difficulty may be faulty; but we have no evidence that this is so. The poets he blames specifically, Eliot and Pound, do have elements in their poetry that are unnecessarily obscure. As for the scholarly study of poetry, some of Larkin's critical remarks show that he supports it rather than the reverse. In a review of an edition of Christina Rossetti's letters to her publisher, he hopes that 'all British publishers will regard their correspondence files as valuable archives for scholars'. He regrets that the scholarly apparatus is inadequate in a review of an edition of *The Collected Poems of William Barnes*. He has contributed some of his manuscripts to the British Museum's collection, and even written an essay for the catalogue of an exhibition of contemporary poets' manuscripts. In his essay, Larkin expresses a hope that contemporary literature will become more recognised as a field of research in British universities, and that British libraries will buy the manuscripts of contemporary poets rather than let them be sold abroad.

Larkin's concern is not that poetry be read merely for pleasure, but lest study by the 'dutiful mob' replace poetry's enjoyment by the wider audience. Such study is 'no substitute' for that enjoyment; but it is not wrong in itself. The critics are damaging only when they abstract poetry from life. 'What I do feel a bit rebellious about,' Larkin has said in a conversation with Ian Hamilton, 'is that poetry seems to have got into the hands of a critical industry which is concerned with culture in the abstract, and this I do rather lay at the door of Eliot and Pound.'[39] We must note again that Larkin objects to 'culture in the abstract', not to culture; indeed, he wishes to see 'culture' in its narrower sense restored to its place in our 'culture' as a whole.

Larkin considers poetry 'an emotional business',[40] which should be a natural part of life (keeping 'the child from its television set and the old man from his pub'), and should take its content directly from what he has called 'unsorted experience'. Consciously or unconsciously, Larkin may have been thinking of a phrase of Hardy's here: 'Unadjusted impressions,' Hardy said in his 1901 preface to *Poems of the Past and Present*, and I take his meaning to be much the same as Larkin's, 'have their value, and the road to a true philosophy of life seems to lie in humbly recording diverse readings of its phenomena as they are forced upon us by chance and change.'[41] Larkin's poems seem to be a record of his agreement with this.

Larkin has never elevated his beliefs about poetry into a system. 'Chance and change' have formed them, as they seem to have formed his feelings about life generally; and that they are expressed only incidentally, in reviewing another's work, or in introducing his own, shows that they are formulated by his writing and reading, not before them. I would stress that one of the strengths of *XX Poems* over his earlier verse was just this: that he did not work to a preconceived ideal of how to write. 'Simply the thing I am shall make me live,' says Parolles. We might adapt the words, and say that Larkin's style and tone and choice of subject matter simply come from the thing he is. The beliefs I outline above are practically exemplified in *XX Poems*, and more so in the third collection, *The Less Deceived*, published four years later. The latter also incorporated a group of five poems published in 1954 as a Fantasy Press pamphlet. Of the poems in the pamphlet, two had already appeared in *XX Poems*: 'If, My Darling' and 'At Grass'.

Though Larkin normally scorns poetic 'development' as a rather artificial, critics' notion, he would probably not argue

39. 'Four Conversations', p. 71.
40. 'Betjeman en Bloc', p. 15.
41. *Collected Poems*, p. 75.

that his poetry 'developed' between *The North Ship* and *XX Poems*. It developed, in the sense that it improved, changed, and took its starting points from a different place. But there is also 'development'—of a kind—between *XX Poems* and *The Less Deceived*. Between the publication of *XX Poems* and *The Less Deceived*, or even *Fantasy Press: Pamphlet 21*, in so far as five poems are able to give an indication, he had recognised the manner and form in which he wrote most effectively. It is no accident that these three publications should all end with the same poem: 'At Grass'. Larkin wanted each collection to have a good final curtain, of course, and 'At Grass' is a very good poem. But more significant, of all the poems in *XX Poems*, 'At Grass' comes nearest to fulfilling those beliefs about poetry outlined above. All my sources for these beliefs are prose pieces published since 1955. In *XX Poems*, 'At Grass' is the poem that derives most obviously from actual experience, and is best able to bear the generalisation that the experience implies. Moreover, in the second edition of *The North Ship*, the poem Larkin added to make a contrast with those published originally in his first collection is similar in kind to 'At Grass'. In fact, it is the poem most similar in conception to 'At Grass' in *XX Poems*. In short, Larkin would have been capable of writing 'Church Going', a great poem and the best in *The Less Deceived*, in 1951: 'At Grass' shows that he had evolved the manner and the technical expertise. He did not write it then, because at that time he had not realised that poems like 'At Grass', rooted firmly in 'unsorted experience', were his most effective. In all the poems of *XX Poems*, Larkin shows an 'obsession with an "emotional concept"' such as he describes as the first stage in the writing of a poem in his essay 'The Pleasure Principle'; but only in 'At Grass' and poems like it, poems founded on concrete particulars, does the emotional concept find its full expression.

The most characteristic poems of *XX Poems* are in fact poems that take an emotional concept, and express it by fleshing it out with an extended metaphor; they are a kind of conceit. Of the poems reprinted in *The Less Deceived*, 'Dry-Point', 'Next Please', 'No Road', and 'Wires' are all of this type: of the poems of *The Less Deceived* that did not appear previously in *XX Poems*, none is like this.

'Next Please' opens with a statement of the emotional concept with which it is concerned:

> Always too eager for the future, we
> Pick up bad habits of expectancy.[42]

The poem goes on to elaborate the concept through a metaphor. We watch for the future in much the same way as someone might watch for ships from a cliff, or, to use the poem's word, a 'bluff'. The word is intended to carry both its meanings here: a promontory, but also a pretence. As we watch, the ships approach like hopes—slowly, but growing clearer all the time. In the poem, the ships are glittering sailing vessels, with ornamented figureheads—the objects of our desires are always more attractive before they are realised. When they are realised they begin to pale; the ships reach us, but do not anchor. They turn, and recede once more into the distance. Larkin is making the point that our hopes are never fulfilled, but that, when they are fulfilled, the fulfilment is only temporary. Fulfilment, in the words of another poem, is often a 'desolate attic',[43] and the reason lies as much in the structure of time itself as in our feelings. Present time is instantaneous.

'Wires' is similar in conception. It is a poem about maturing, which works like an animal fable: cattle learn in the same way as we. However wide the pasture, the poem suggests, it has wires which enclose it, and though old cattle know better through experience, the young ones always try to transgress the electric fence:

> Beyond the wires

> Leads them to blunder up against the wires
> Whose muscle-shredding violence gives no quarter.[44]

The young cattle learn their limitations through pain. The poem itself enacts the limitations: it is in two stanzas of four lines each. There is no rhyme within each stanza, but the rhyme scheme of

42. *T.L.D.*, p. 20.
43. 'Deceptions', *T.L.D.*, p. 37.
44. *T.L.D.*, p. 27.

the second stanza is a mirror image of that of the first, so that the last line of the poem rhymes with the first, the next last with the second, and so on, abcd dcba. Like the electric fence, the rhymes gradually close round until the circle is complete

There is no feeling in either of the poems I discuss above that the objects are real. In 'Next Please', the ships described are not such as we would see if we really watched from a cliff, and in 'Wires' we have no feeling of the actuality of the cattle. This is not the case in another animal poem in *The Less Deceived*, 'Myxomatosis', in which the poet comes across a rabbit suffering from the disease in a field, and kills it, to save it further pain. Both 'Wires' and 'Myxomatosis' are about suffering: the first treats of the way suffering matures the sufferer, the second of our inability to reach across the suffering of another creature to offer real comfort. The great difference between the two poems is that 'Wires' is an intellectual apprehension of an emotional concept and no more, but 'Myxomatosis' is realised emotionally as well as intellectually. We immediately feel sorry for the rabbit, in fact, and sympathise with the speaker's inability to comfort the suffering animal; whereas our feelings for the cattle in 'Wires' are neither here nor there.

'Myxomatosis' seems to me a better poem than 'Wires' because in the latter the conception is quite abstract, and there is no reality to conduct any emotional charge. Consequently, there is no such charge. In 'Myxomatosis' emotions are generated, concentrated and directed because they run through a particular, realised event. I hesitate to introduce the phrase, bearing in mind Larkin's feeling that in some ways, T. S. Eliot has done some disservice to English poetry, but 'Myxomatosis' gives us an 'objective correlative' for the emotions, whereas 'Wires' does not. Though 'Wires' makes a larger statement than 'Myxomatosis', the more limited one is of greater value. In 'Wires' we are merely presented with a generalisation: it is rather like being given the answer to a mathematical problem without any of the mechanics of its solution. The poet might have made a lucky guess, or been told the answer by someone else. But in 'Myxomatosis' we see all the working, so to speak: we are confident that the solution is not just haphazard, but derived from experience.

Perhaps pieces like 'Wires' owe their relative failure to the fact that the correspondences of metaphor and concept are detailed too coldly. The metaphor itself seems arbitrary, except in so far as it is able to illustrate the ramifications of the concept. The resultant poem is too much like an exercise. The conclusion of 'Next Please' contrasts strongly with the rest of the poem. In this, by far the most striking part of the poem, Larkin says that though we constantly watch for 'our ship to come in':

> Only one ship is seeking us, a black-
> Sailed unfamiliar, towing at her back
> A huge and birdless silence. In her wake
> No waters breed or break.[45]

The great difference between this and the rest of the poem is that in the first part, as in 'Wires' as a whole and in other poems of a similar kind, like 'No Road', we are impressed by how aptly the metaphor illustrates the concept; but at the end of 'Next Please', we feel that the metaphor is really indistinguishable from the concept it illustrates. The metaphor embodies the concept, rather than describes it; the difference is rather like that between an illustrative diagram and a painting in which the artist has been emotionally and intellectually involved.

When Larkin's poems do strive after a universal statement, they work best when they grow out of the kind of experience Larkin evokes in 'Myxomatosis'. His themes are almost always personal or perennial ones, and he is sometimes criticised for not writing about the impact of such specifically contemporary phenomena as Hiroshima and Auschwitz. 'That millions in the world are really, and horribly, suffering seems not to inhibit the complaints one whit',[46] said an American critic, M. L. Rosenthal, accusing Larkin and poets like him of being moved solely by the petty discomforts of living in welfare-state England. Before he took a more obvious stance, Emerson was asked why he had made no pronouncement against slavery, and he replied that he did not need to: anyone who read his works could see that he

45. *T.L.D.*, p. 20.
46. M. L. Rosenthal, 'Tuning in on Albion', *The Nation*, 16 May 1959, p. 457.

would not support the system. Something similar may be said of Larkin's work. He is a contemporary man, and his observation of life is deeply influenced by the phenomena of contemporary life; but these things are part of the texture of his vision. He does not need to write about them directly to show that he is aware of them. A. Alvarez over-simplifies Larkin's responses in 'Beyond the Gentility Principle'. He condemns the Movement poets as 'genteel', portraying them as neo-Georgians, unconcerned with the terrifying aspects of contemporary life, resolutely turning away from such uncomfortable facts as suicide and insanity, with which Robert Lowell, Sylvia Plath and John Berryman strive, on the page, to come to terms.

Specifically, Alvarez invites us to compare Larkin's 'At Grass' with Ted Hughes's 'A Dream of Horses'. He does not actually say that Hughes's poem is better, but he does say that each poem allows a different 'kind of success'. Hughes's poem is more 'urgent'—a value-laden term in the context of this essay—and his praise of Larkin's poem is patronising: it is 'rather beautiful in its gentle way'.[47] Since Alvarez is trying to illustrate what he means by 'gentility', a quality that prevents some contemporary poems from having any real importance, he is implying that not only is the success of Larkin's poem of a different kind, but of an inferior one as well.

Alvarez is entitled to his opinion, but the method he uses to persuade others to his view, that Hughes's poem is more important than Larkin's, is suspect. He compares the objects in each poem, suggesting that 'At Grass' is less worthy of notice because the horses in it are less frightening than those in 'A Dream of Horses'. 'At Grass,' Alvarez says, is 'a nostalgic re-creation of the Platonic (or *New Yorker*) idea of the English scene, part pastoral, part sporting.'[48] In other words, what kind of 'success' is it that sees England as an American glossy magazine might? But if Alvarez had compared the portrait of the retired racehorses in 'At Grass' to those in a painting by George Stubbs, say, he would have given a quite different impression, as well as being nearer the truth. Hughes's poem, he points out, is 'undoubtedly *about* something', and the implication seems to be that Larkin's is not, or

47. 'Beyond the Gentility Principle', p. 30.
48. *Ibid.*

at least, not about anything of importance; but in fact the experience of watching horses in 'At Grass' provides Larkin with a starting point, from which he can imply certain feelings about time and anonymity. It is not 'about' horses in the same way as Dr Spock's *Baby and Child Care* is 'about' babies.

Larkin watched these particular horses at one remove, on a newsreel film of Brown Jack, the racehorse, in his retirement. Being racehorses, they had had glamorous lives, but now they are bothered only by wind and flies. The poet wonders if memories of the past 'plague their ears', and evokes the horses' past, a scene of fifteen years previously:

> Silks at the start: against the sky
> Numbers and parasols: outside,
> Squadrons of empty cars, and heat,
> And littered grass:[49]

The lines describe the scene, but the change in metre makes us hear and see it. Where the other stanzas are written in iambic pentameters, reversals of feet in this third stanza turn the first halves of these three lines into rocking choriambics, enacting the horses' gallop.

We must conclude that if memories do plague the horses' ears, they do not regret the passing of their glory. Now their names live only in almanacs:

> they

> Have slipped their names, and stand at ease,
> Or gallop for what must be joy,

Their anonymity is perhaps a model of the oblivion we desire, according to Larkin's 'Wants', and which 'runs just under all we do', for in the speaker's words there is a kind of envy of the withdrawal from life that these horses have achieved. Besides presenting the life of two retired racehorses, 'At Grass' dramatises the attitudes of the speaker.

Alvarez is right: 'At Grass' is a pastoral poem, and it celebrates withdrawal from the insistent pressures of contemporary life,

49. *T.L.D.*, p. 45.

rather than urges us to confront them. This is Alvarez's chief objection to the poem, an objection amplified by Charles Tomlinson when he accuses Larkin of a 'retreat behind the privet hedge'. But such criticisms take insufficient notice of the poem's tone. If we compare 'At Grass' with other, earlier pastorals that celebrate such a withdrawal, we see an obvious difference. Here is a stanza from Cowper's 'On Solitude':

> Hail, the pure muse's richest manor seat!
>   Ye country houses and retreat,
>   Which all the happy gods so love
> That for you oft they quit their light and great
>   Metropolis above.

Cowper's poem is joyful, a paean to natural beauty and the delights of being alone in the unspoilt countryside. Larkin's is elegiac and melancholy: there is a feeling that for humankind, the idyllic life the horses enjoy is no longer possible. If Fielding were writing today, he could not set Squire Allworthy in a Paradise Hall. Pomfret describes the ideal pastoral life in *The Choice*: it is meditative, spent with a congenial companion on a modest income in an unpretentious, though well-situated house in the country. The house has a garden, an adequate library, and a small wine cellar. 'A system of life,' said Dr Johnson of this ideal, 'adapted to common notions, and equal to common expectations.' He could not say so today. Even as recently as 1914, when E. M. Forster finished *Maurice*, his novel about the homosexual love of a young man for a social inferior, it was not ridiculous to suggest that they could withdraw from society into rural England to avoid opprobrium. When the book was published, in 1970, this withdrawal no longer seemed feasible, and reviewers found the conclusion of the book hard to accept. In the second half of the twentieth century, in order to postulate such a pastoral retreat as Fielding or Pomfret postulate, or the kind of anonymity within it achieved at the end of *Maurice* by the homosexual lovers, Larkin cannot refer to people. This is the knowledge that informs the poem, and makes it melancholy. We are able to imagine the ideal, but it is no longer within our expectations.

Perhaps the most exaggerated example of the kind of simplification Alvarez makes was uttered by Dame Edith Sitwell, when she complained in a letter to the *Times Literary Supplement* that poetry no longer seemed to be the study of Man, as it concerned itself only with 'troubles about bicycle clips'. She is referring, of course, to 'Church Going', which I shall discuss later. Her point is valid to the extent that Larkin's poems often do start from very small beginnings: hearing a jazz record, the sight of a children's playground at four o'clock, the sound of a ship's hooter, looking at a girl's photographs. Just as he chose to end three collections with the same poem, Larkin opened *Fantasy Press: Pamphlet 21* and *The Less Deceived* with one poem: 'Lines on a Young Lady's Photograph Album'. It is like 'At Grass' in starting from a particular experience which is recreated on the page.

'Lines on a Young Lady's Photograph Album' has a literary antecedent in C. Day Lewis's 'The Album'. Both poems start from the experience of looking at snapshots in an album, both poems are addressed to the subject of the photographs, and both lead to a reflection on how the past affects us in the present. There is no other similarity, but a comparison of the two poems may bring out the qualities of Larkin's. The great difference between the two is in their organising principles. Day Lewis's poem, besides being about looking in a photograph album, is about the relationships he has had with two women. The first is the subject of the photographs, a woman he loved, and who loved him. He describes photographs that picture her at various ages, and to each description he adds a comment on how he wishes he could warn her about what she will become in the final photograph. She is pictured at all stages except the last, which would show her when the love that joined her to the poet had withered. But though he regrets the past, he is consoled by the present, and the second woman:

> I close the book;
> But the past slides out of its leaves to haunt me
> And it seems, wherever I look,
> Phantoms of irreclaimable happiness taunt me.
> Then I see her, petalled in new-blown hours,
> Beside me—'All you love most there

> Has blossomed again,' she murmurs, 'all that you
>   missed there
> Has grown to be yours.'[50]

The elegiac, regretful mood is sustained throughout, even in this last stanza, when his new loved one reassures him about his present—she 'murmurs' to suit the mood.

The poem is unified by the metaphors and similes, and the objects in each photograph: the girl is always surrounded by flowers. In the reversal in the fourth stanza, when the poet reveals the failure of his love, he pictures the woman as a stripped tree, without the fruit that the blossom had promised. And in the last stanza, he is reassured that there is new blossom in his love, and even what he had previously missed has 'grown'. Day Lewis erects a scaffolding of metaphors to keep the poem together—it is artificial, though not in any pejorative sense of that word.

Larkin's poem works in quite a different way. There is no detailed description in 'Lines on a Young Lady's Photograph Album' as there is in 'The Album', no attempt to imitate the photograph in words. Larkin recreates not the photographs, but the experience of looking at the photographs in the presence of the young lady. The poem is dramatic. This is apparent not only in the unspoken asides to the girl, and in the explicit directions to this or that photograph, but in the way the poem constantly shifts tone and mood. We are convinced not that the poet has brought a mood to the experience, but that the experience is actively shaping his mood.

At first, he is light, joking with the girl, protesting in the manner of the courtly lover that the photographs are:

> Too much confectionery, too rich:
> I choke on such nutritious images.[51]

When he sees a picture of the girl in a trilby hat, he comments, in a vaguely sexual innuendo, 'Faintly disturbing, that, in

50. C. Day Lewis, 'The Album', *Selected Poems*, expanded edition, Harmondsworth 1969, p. 95.
51. *T.L.D.*, p. 13.

several ways', and, noticing that there are young men in certain of the photos, he says, mock-pompously, 'Not quite your class, I'd say, dear, on the whole.' 'Sweet girl graduate' is an echo from Tennyson's 'medley', 'The Princess', where Lilia, a vociferous and very pretty supporter of women's emancipation, describes the college she would establish, given the chance. An indulgent but patronising man lightly replies that with 'sweet girl graduates in their golden hair' academic processions might become fashion parades. Larkin goes on to apostrophise photography, addressing the art as a muse:

> But o, photography! as no art is,
> Faithful and disappointing!

Disappointing *because* faithful—he sees that the photograph holds the past moment with all its imperfections,

> And will not censor blemishes
> Like washing-lines, and Hall's-Distemper boards,

But the prosaic actuality jars against the elevated language of the address, and seems to pull the speaker up short. As if taken by surprise, he stops turning the pages of the album, and reflects that the photographs are really affecting. He asks why. Is it because of their very actuality—'Or is it just *the past*?' By means of the question, and the 'Yes, true,' in the next stanza, the movement of the speaker's mind is recreated.

The mood has settled, and the rest of the poem maintains a constant, serious tone, with none of the play-acting of the first half. The poem becomes a serious reflection on the past's effect on our present. It is affecting because it is simply past: he senses the mortality implicit in all our actions and memories of them. Seen at one level, 'Life is slow dying,' Larkin says in one poem, and these photographs are a perpetual reminder that time is constantly passing:

> Those flowers, that gate,
> These misty parks and motors, lacerate
> Simply by being over;

But more than this, Larkin reflects, such images of the past move us because they indulge our grief without questioning it. Most things that engage our emotions in the present have consequences of some kind, but the fact that the past is unreachable means that we are prompted in no such way. The poet can risk an emotional engagement with the girl in the photograph, whereas the girl who stands before him may make demands he cannot fulfil. Or, perhaps, as he can contain her past through the photographs, he can be sure of it; of her future, he cannot be so certain. He can 'condense'

> a past that no one now can share,
> No matter whose your future;[52]

I shall single out two other poems from *The Less Deceived* which work in a similar way to 'Lines on a Young Lady's Photograph Album' and 'At Grass'. The first, 'I Remember, I Remember', deserves specific consideration because, besides being the kind of poem most often associated with Larkin, it illustrates his superb craftsmanship. The second is 'Church Going', which demands detailed treatment because it is arguably Larkin's best poem, and undoubtedly his best known, most anthologised, and most discussed.

Like 'Lines on a Young Lady's Photograph Album', 'I Remember, I Remember' has a literary antecedent—though both poems arise from experiences other than literary ones. In this case, the antecedent, Hood's poem of the same name, is indicated in the title. Hood sentimentally contrasts an idyllic world of childhood with a miserable maturity:

> I remember, I remember,
> The house where I was born,
> The little window where the sun
> Came peeping in at morn;
> He never came a wink too soon,
> Nor brought too long a day,
> But now, I often wish the night
> Had borne my breath away!

52. *T.L.D.*, p. 14.

For Hood, it was always summer when he was a child; the sun always shone, though never so fiercely that it woke him rudely, and there was always a breeze, to prevent the heat from becoming oppressive. Such words as 'little' and 'peeping' are syrupy in this context. It might be argued that Larkin too is sentimental, though sentimental at the other end of the scale, in making his childhood seem so dismal. But again, we must reflect that Larkin's poem is not about his childhood in the same sense as Hood's is. Larkin's 'I Remember, I Remember' is about just that—remembering. It is about the experience of looking back at childhood on a particular occasion. We have no evocations of what happened, or what his childhood home looked like. At that moment, when the train in which the poet is making a journey north, taking an unusual diversion, stops at Coventry, his birth-place, he can remember only what did not happen. His childhood contained none of the unusual formative incidents usually recounted in literary autobiographies or autobiographical novels.

One commentator has suggested that the things that did not happen are 'curiously similar to some of those in *Sons and Lovers*'.[53] This is true, but not curious, surely. If Larkin wanted to remind us of an autobiographical novel, *Sons and Lovers* is surely a fairly obvious choice. And in fact, Larkin read Lawrence avidly as an adolescent. I think Larkin did not intend us to turn to the book, however; he merely wanted to give the feel of such books as *Portrait of the Artist as a Young Man* (or *as a Young Dog*), *Look Homeward, Angel*, and *Cider With Rosie*. The words in quotation marks in the sixth stanza do not direct us to a particular novel: they are an all-purpose cliché, or long-hand ellipsis marks.

In fact, it is not true that Larkin can remember nothing of his childhood. In a short piece with a title taken from his poem, 'Not the Place's Fault', which Larkin wrote for *Umbrella*, a Coventry arts magazine of very limited circulation, now defunct, he recounts some fascinating memories of his childhood. True, none would have appeared in a *Sons and Lovers* kind of autobiographical novel—but that is the point the poem makes. The

53. A. Kingsley Weatherhead, 'Philip Larkin of England', *ELH*, XXXVIII (December 1971), p. 624.

'THE LESS DECEIVED'

friend with whom the poet is travelling notes the bitterness in his face as he reflects on his 'unspent' childhood:

> 'You look as if you wished the place in Hell,'
> My friend said, 'judging from your face.' 'Oh well,
> I suppose it's not the place's fault,' I said.

> 'Nothing, like something, happens anywhere.'[54]

The last line is immensely powerful, partly owing to its felicitous phrasing, but more to its honesty. How often have we heard someone deride his birthplace? Larkin will not flatter himself by settling the shortcomings of his childhood on the place where it was spent. The line finishes the poem in completing its form, as well as being physically the last words. Though typographically tacked on to the end of the poem, the final line completes a complex, large scale rhyme scheme, which breaks across the seven-line stanzas. By rhyme, the poem is in four units, each unit having three rhymes—abccbaabc. The rhyme scheme, by joining stanza to stanza—there is no point at which the end of a rhyme unit and the end of a stanza coincide—unifies the poem.

In view of the complexity of this rhyme scheme, a complexity increased by its marriage to the stanza scheme, it is astonishing that Larkin has been able to make the tone of the poem so straightforwardly conversational, and even more so that he can report convincing dialogue. In his preface to *Lyrical Ballads*, Wordsworth argued for a poetic diction that should be drawn from the spoken language of the day. His practice did not fully follow his theory; but here, Larkin perfectly achieves an idiom that is living and contemporary. And he does this without lapsing into flatness, as that marvellous last line proves.

The same is true of 'Church Going', which combines and brings to consummation the virtues of the poems I have been discussing above. It is certainly a central poem in Larkin's work, and is as important a statement of the mid-twentieth century consciousness as Arnold's 'Dover Beach' was of the mid-nineteenth. In a widely-read survey of modern literature, *The Modern Writer and his World*, G. S. Fraser called 'Church Going' 'the Movement's prize poem . . . a poem with claims to greatness'. It is certainly

54. *T.L.D.*, p. 39.

the best and most important poem in *New Lines*, and it certainly
has claims to greatness; but it is not the Movement's prize poem
in the sense of being the best poem in the Movement manner.
There is no 'neutral tone' in this poem, and no avoidance of the
grand theme; 'Church Going' cannot be defined by negatives.
But perhaps, as a *Times Literary Supplement* correspondent said in
an article on 'The State of Poetry' in 1958, the best poems of any
movement are often those that will not fit its theoretical mould.
The preface to *Lyrical Ballads* will not account for 'Tintern Abbey'
or 'The Ancient Mariner'. Conquest's introduction to *New Lines*
does not explain this magnificent final stanza:

> A serious house on serious earth it is,
> In whose blent air all our compulsions meet,
> Are recognised, and robed as destinies.
> And that much never can be obsolete,
> Since someone will forever be surprising
> A hunger in himself to be more serious,
> And gravitating with it to this ground,
> Which, he once heard, was proper to grow wise in,
> If only that so many dead lie round.[55]

This stanza has a weighty sonorousness: the alliteration within
the lines, the careful balance of each around the caesura, the
slightly heightened diction, and above all the measured stresses
of the metre—here, all the lines are end-stopped by punctuation
or by sense—emphasise the seriousness, to use the poem's word,
of the conclusion. No other poem in the Movement anthologies
seriously adopts this diction, is so emphatic in its statement, or
uses such words as 'forever' or 'destinies' without satirical intent.
The final stanza is an unreserved affirmation of the importance
of the central events in human life: the seriousness of the church
derives from the fact that it has:

> held unspilt
> So long and equably what since is found
> Only in separation—marriage, and birth,
> And death, and thoughts of these—

55. *T.L.D.*, p. 29.

The church, a symbol of the unity of these events, may decay, for 'Church Going' means church-going in the normal sense, casually visiting a church, and the going of the church; but if it falls into ruin, life will be poorer for it. Even in this case, though, Larkin feels that the place will lure people, for we have a 'hunger' for what it represents, which will take us there, though unwittingly; and in fact, just this has happened to the speaker of the poem. The last stanza is the solution to the problem the poet poses himself at the beginning. Out for a bicycle ride, the poet stops at a church, and goes in to look round. He mocks what the church connotes for him, but in the face of this, thinks that something did make him stop. That something, he finally realises, is 'a hunger to be serious', which is satisfied by this building and and what it truly represents. The final statement is the more convincing in being made by an agnostic.

As in 'Myxomatosis', this conclusion is convincing because it is worked for. Larkin does not produce a pious sentiment out of his hat: he dramatises the movement of the speaker's mind in coming to his conclusion. He does this by evoking successive emotions through variations in tone. As I noted with regard to 'Lines on a Young Lady's Photograph Album', Larkin's ability to shift convincingly from tone to tone within a single poem is startling: few poets are able in one poem to produce the curt, dismissive colloquialism of 'Some ruin-bibber, randy for antique' and the first two lines of the last stanza, without destroying its unity. To return to the opening of this book, it is an ability shared by Andrew Marvell: think of the subtle modulations in 'To His Coy Mistress' where the humorous hyperbole of

> My vegetable Love should grow
> Vaster then Empires, and more slow.

can change to the tone of these justly famous lines:

> But at my back I alwaies hear
> Times winged Chariot hurrying near:

with no intrusive or unnatural break.

When the speaker first enters the church, he makes a brief,

impressionistic and rather contemptuous assessment of its contents.
It is just 'Another church':

> matting, seats, and stone,
> And little books; sprawlings of flowers, cut
> For Sunday, brownish now; some brass and stuff
> Up at the holy end;[56]

The description is deliberately inexact, telling us more about him
than the church. 'Church Going' is like 'I Remember, I Remember' in being about a person's feelings, thoughts and emotions
in a particular situation, not just about what he can see and hear.
The poem is not about churches directly, but about a certain
man, with a certain disposition, visiting a church at a certain
time.

He walks around to the font, looks at the large bible, and
parodies the manner of the vicar or lay reader. But having done
so, he finds he has emotions that remain unsatisfied: he feels
that there is something he has missed, but he cannot quite see
what it is. He stopped at the church, he went in, he mildly
ridiculed the connotations of the place—but why did he stop
at all?

> Yet stop I did: in fact I often do,
> And always end much at a loss like this,
> Wondering what to look for;

He cannot have stopped for the shabby flowers, the musty hymn
books, the big bible; but these things have their function in the
poem. They are what the church contains—but they are only
its visible contents. They contrast with the more important things
the church has 'held unspilt' for so long: births, marriages and
deaths, which are its real history.

At first, the speaker does not realise this, but begins to reflect
on what will happen 'When churches fall completely out of use.'
His mood is still jocular. Perhaps the church plate may be kept
on show (the alliteration of 'parchment, plate and pyx' shows

56. *T.L.D.*, p. 28.

that he is phrase-making), and the rest 'let rent-free to rain and sheep'. In the fourth stanza, his conscious archaism in 'simples', his almost forcing us through the metre to say 'Advisèd', and his later mention of 'cancer' and 'a dead one' show his mood moving through satire to apprehensiveness. Perhaps superstition will still bring people to the place, but even that dies out, he reflects. The literalness of his picture of the church at this stage of its decay shows that he is no longer in a humorous vein.

> And what remains when disbelief has gone?
> Grass, weedy pavement, brambles, buttress, sky,
> A shape less recognisable each week,
> A purpose more obscure.

Wondering who will be the last to come to the church as it stands, he becomes angry. Will it be

> Some ruin-bibber, randy for antique,
> Or Christmas-addict, counting on a whiff
> Of gowns-and-bands and organ-pipes and myrrh? [57]

This is the clue that leads him to the reason why he stopped. Those 'randy for antique' will be looking for incidentals, objects, having no more to do with the true significance of the church than the faded flowers: they are seekers and purveyors of the 'culture in the abstract' that Larkin abhors. Such people, in Eliot's words, will have 'had the experience but missed the meaning'; and that meaning Larkin states in the last two stanzas of the poem.

Speaking of 'Church Going', Larkin said: 'I think one has to dramatise oneself a little.' [58] I have pointed out how this is true of 'Lines on a Young Lady's Photograph Album' as well as 'Church Going', poems that are not generally recognised to be dramatic. Not making such a recognition, or not fully making it, leads to such a mistake as John Press's, in an essay on 'English Verse Since 1945'. Press recognises that the speaker of 'Church Going' is a character, a persona for the poet. But he feels that the character is incredible. How can a man who refers to 'brass and

57. *T.L.D.*, p. 29.
58. Ian Hamilton, 'Four Conversations', p. 74.

stuff/Up at the holy end' be familiar with such terms as 'rood lofts' and 'pyx'? Press seems not to see that 'brass and stuff' is indicative not of the speaker's state of knowledge, but of his attitude. How, Press asks, can a man who is presented as awkward and clumsy ('Hatless, I take off/My cycle clips in awkward reverence') be capable of the splendid peroration?[59] Besides pointing out that the most intelligent and eloquent of men can be made uncomfortable by emotions they do not fully understand, and that there is no indication in the poem that the speaker is clumsy (though even if there were, I see no reason why such an affliction might rule out powers of oratory), we should note that early in the poem, the speaker shows himself to be a man of great verbal inventiveness, even if his object is humorous rather than serious.

Larkin's modulations in tone are often extremely subtle, and it is necessary to read closely to catch all the nuances in a particular poem. Many of his poems are dramatic in the sense that they present a slant view of his opinions, through just such a persona as the one in 'Church Going'. In 'Reasons For Attendance', Larkin plays the academic university librarian, just old enough to feel out of touch with the students with whom he deals. Invited to a student dance, he approaches cautiously, and, peering through a window, sees that this is not the place for him. Sex, 'the wonderful feel of girls'—there is a marvellous lasciviousness in the very vagueness of that phrase, as well as in its drawn-out vowels and alliterated 'l's—is an attraction, perhaps, but he is drawn to Art, rather than this 'maul to and fro'. The pompous dismissiveness of this phrase is belied by the more genuine, if baser, emotion conveyed by the first I quote. But we appreciate the hollowness of his sentiments by the very smugness with which they are expressed:

> Surely, to think the lion's share
> Of happiness is found by couples—sheer

> Inaccuracy, as far as I'm concerned.[60]

59. John Press, 'English Verse Since 1945', *Essays by Divers Hands, XXXI*, London 1962, p. 169.
60. *T.L.D.*, p. 18.

And if Larkin has not already destroyed any confidence we might have had in the speaker's pose by the grandiosity of 'What calls me is that lifted, rough-tongued bell', he certainly does so with his Late-Night-Line-Up litotes, which ostensibly disclaims the grandiosity, but in fact compounds it: 'Art, if you like.' It is worth noting that this is the only occasion on which Larkin mentions the fact that he is a poet in the whole of his mature work. At the end of the poem, Larkin breaks in in his authentic voice:

> I stay outside,
> Believing this; and they maul to and fro,
> Believing that; and both are satisfied,
> If no one has misjudged himself. Or lied.

The final words of the poem work like those of 'Poetry of Departures'. In that poem, the speaker wonders about his life, and questions why he does not break with it:

> Yes, swagger the nut-strewn roads,
> Crouch in the fo'c'sle
> Stubbly with goodness,[61]

His language, and the picture he evokes, call to my mind the stories and illustrations I read as a boy, *Wizard* and *Hotspur* (still in existence, but now much changed). They show that he is unconvinced by such day-dreams, though sympathetic to the dreamers, for he is one himself. He cannot afford to feel superior in his recognition of their artificiality, however, for his life may be reduced to ornaments:

> Books; china; a life
> Reprehensibly perfect.

Here, and at the end of 'Reasons For Attendance', as Ian Hamilton has said, 'the tongue is removed from the cheek and given a sharp bite.'[62]

Reviewing *The Less Deceived* and Betjeman's *Collected Poems*

61. *T.L.D.*, p. 34.
62. Ian Hamilton, 'Poetry', *London Magazine*, IV (Summer 1964), p. 71.

for an American periodical, M. L. Rosenthal suggested that the major characteristic of Larkin's poetry is a '*petty* bitterness about life' deriving from the poet's own self-pity: 'The tragic and revolutionary perspectives of the great generation of modern poets begin to seem archaic to people embroiled in the petty particulars of welfare-state planning. Most of their passion goes into self-loathing at being part of a protected, routine system of minimum standards and into indignation that Albion's sacred landscape is being "modernised".'[63] A. Alvarez made a similar point when he rather backhandedly complimented Larkin for his 'main achievement': to have created 'a special voice'[64] for welfare-state England. Edmund Crispin once said that he could not agree with those who see Larkin as a sort of 'Parnassian Ron Glum'; nor can I. Rosenthal in particular, and Alvarez to some extent, either dismiss or just fail to recognise those features of *The Less Deceived* that violently militate against this view.

I have pointed out that Larkin's themes are not petty, but rather the reverse. Poems are often specifically about conditions of life that are applicable in any time. 'Triple Time', for instance, a poem about our view of the present from the past, from the future, and in the present itself, deals with Time, not time in post-war provincial England. Rosenthal does not recognise Larkin's intense feeling for natural beauty, as it is illustrated in 'At Grass', or his frequent moments of lyricism, like this from 'Maiden Name', when he reflects on what a woman's maiden name means to him, now she is married:

> It means what we feel now about you then:
> How beautiful you were, and near, and young,
> So vivid, you might still be there among
> Those first few days, unfingermarked again.[65]

He takes no account of 'Wedding Wind', spoken by a woman in joyful celebration of her recent marriage, or the almost knock-about humour of 'Toads' and its sequel, 'Toads Revisited'. Death and age, two of Larkin's most obsessive themes, come to

63. 'Tuning in on Albion', p. 457.
64. 'Philip Larkin', in *Beyond All This Fiddle*, p. 85.
65. *T.L.D.*, p. 23.

us whether we have grown up in post- or pre-war England. Is the voice in 'Wants', in 'Age', in 'Days', in 'Absences' the voice of a poet venting, in Rosenthal's words, 'a querulous whine', or in Alvarez's, a 'voice for a special, localized moment'? Far from showing an obsession with himself, 'Absences' suggests Larkin's exhilaration at the prospect of a place that is entirely innocent of him:

> Such attics cleared of me! Such absences![66]

Asked to pick one of his poems for an American anthology called *Poet's Choice*, Larkin picked 'Absences', saying 'I am always thrilled by the thought of what places look like when I am not there.'[67]

It is true that Larkin sees life as limiting, and that he believes the limits close in on us as we age. But what prevents our fulfilment in life is not merely the petty difficulties and shabbinesses of contemporary Britain; it is, in the words of 'Dockery and Son', 'something hidden from us', an unidentifiable. One of the best poems in *The Less Deceived*, 'Arrivals, Departures', identifies the 'something' with the sound of a ship's horn. The horn blows in the morning when it brings the traveller into the docks, and wakes the townspeople to 'Horny dilemmas'. 'Horny', though a regrettable pun, perhaps, combines the notion of a ship's horn, which makes the sound of cattle, 'lowing', with the uncomfortable trials of the day ahead for those it wakes. It is a note of disaster: onomatopoeically, it says 'Come and choose wrong' in the morning, and 'O not for long' at evening, as it again 'nudges' the townspeople from 'comfort'. The sound of a ship's horn is a perfect expression of a feeling of desolation that cannot be explained. There is no doubt that it does make us feel this desolation, whether we put words to the sound or not; but we are at a loss to explain why.

Perhaps Rosenthal's objections seem most reasonable in the case of poems like 'Born Yesterday', which was written for Kingsley Amis's daughter, Sally. Here, it may appear that

66. *T. L. D.*, p. 40.
67. Philip Larkin, 'Absences', in *Poet's Choice*, ed. Paul Engel and Joseph Langland, New York 1962, p. 202.

Larkin is justifying G. S. Fraser's objection to his poetry: Larkin's view is diminishing, Fraser says, in that for Larkin, the sensible man (or woman, in this poem) settles for second-bests.[68] The poem is reminiscent of Yeats's 'A Prayer For My Daughter'. To my knowledge, Yeats has not been castigated for his hope that his daughter should not be too beautiful or too intelligent—he knew too well what agonies a beautiful, self-opinionated woman can cause—but this is only what Larkin wishes. Fraser's objection rests on such wishes as this:

> May you be ordinary;
> Have, like other women,
> An average of talents:[69]

This, says Larkin, is a wish for Sally Amis to be 'dull'; but he goes on to define this dullness as a 'skilled/Vigilant, flexible/Unemphasised, enthralled/Catching of happiness'. If our lives are largely determined by 'something hidden from us', the little girl could not choose to be dull, nor to be happy. Such things are not a question of free will, of 'settling' for the inferior or undemanding.

A younger poet than Larkin, Philip Hobsbaum, has assessed his importance to contemporary poetry:

> Round about 1950, in the worst doldrums English
> verse has ever known, Larkin was the first poet to write
> poems that looked like poetry: that had shape, plot,
> scene, argument, and yet were incontestably of our
> time.[70]

As a matter of fact, it was round about 1946, for that was when 'Wedding Wind', the earliest poem in *The Less Deceived*, was written. But the volume has more than merely historical interest. Larkin showed in *The Less Deceived* that he did not write poetry

68. G. S. Fraser, 'The Poetry of Thom Gunn', *Critical Quarterly*, III (Winter 1961), p. 359.

69. *T.L.D.*, p. 24.

70. Philip Hobsbaum, 'Where Are the War Poets?', *Outposts*, 61 (Summer 1964), p. 23.

that blows off the top of one's head, to use Emily Dickinson's metaphor; but the collection did show that he wrote movingly and memorably about aspects of life that were of great importance to his readers as well as to himself. He showed that he was a witty poet with immense verbal facility, capable of the most subtle modulations of tone, speaking a language vitalised by its relationship with the idiom we speak. He showed above all, to use his own phrases, that he was a poet 'capable of strong feeling' and 'of conveying strong feeling in poetry'.[71]

71. 'No More Fever', p. 24.

5   *The Whitsun Weddings*

The Whitsun Weddings was published by Faber and Faber in 1964. It was almost nine years since Larkin's previous collection and the new one was welcomed by both reviewers and public. The *Times Literary Supplement* and the *New York Review of Books*, the most widely read organs of literary opinion in Britain and the U.S.A., praised it highly. The *Times Literary Supplement* approvingly quoted Kenneth Allott's comment from the *Penguin Book of Contemporary Verse*: Larkin is 'the most exciting new poetic voice—with the possible exception of Dylan Thomas—since Auden'. The reviewer for the *New York Review of Books*, Professor Christopher Ricks, is British, but Americans also thought the collection a considerable achievement. A rather slick piece in *Time* magazine said: 'If Larkin is not a great poet, he is nevertheless the only British poet who still seems able to compose great poems.' And the influential American critic and poet Louise Bogan added more measured and weighty, if somewhat school report-like praise:

> this member of what is now becoming a middle-aged
> British poetic generation possesses formal gifts that are
> not only perfectly controlled and strongly sustained but
> capable of wide and interesting variation. He is able to
> use such gifts as they are seldom used, to describe the
> tough realities of his time.[1]

When in 1965 *The Whitsun Weddings* won the Queen's Gold Medal for Poetry, Larkin observed with characteristic self-deprecation that Auden had won the medal at the age of thirty; he was forty-two. None the less, it attracted more popular notice than *The Less Deceived* had in 1955, selling 3,800 copies in its first six months—an enormous sale for a volume of new poems by a

1. Louise Bogan, 'Books: Verse', *New Yorker*, 10 April 1965, p. 193.

contemporary poet—and the award of the medal stimulated the interest of the mass-media: Larkin was the subject of a B.B.C. *Monitor* film, of an article in the *Sunday Times Colour Supplement*, and of another in the *Guardian*.

The collection seemed to consolidate the opinion both of Larkin's admirers and his detractors, rather than to make any converts. Certain critics had registered their unease at some aspects of Larkin's poetry, and it seems that *The Whitsun Weddings* made them more uneasy; but one objection was made to it that could not apply to *The Less Deceived*. It makes a good starting point for a discussion of the poems in this fourth collection.

Reviewing *The Whitsun Weddings* for the *Observer*, A. Alvarez said that though Larkin's themes 'may have changed superficially . . . his style has developed not at all'. Francis Hope in *Encounter* echoed the complaint: 'There are no poems here which would look out of place in *The Less Deceived*, and as that was published nine years ago one might say that Mr Larkin was consistent to the point of being static.' Of course, some critics made almost the same observation, but considered this feature of Larkin's work to be a virtue. 'Mr Larkin seems to have arrived all at once where he was going,' D. J. Enright considered in the *New Statesman*, but claimed that Larkin always writes 'like an angel'; and in a very sympathetic piece on Larkin's poetry, Anthony Thwaite has said that Larkin's mature poems 'make a total unified impact': between 'Wedding Wind' and Larkin's most recent work, 'there has been no radical development'.

It is not surprising that at least some of the poems from *The Whitsun Weddings* would appear to fit almost equally well into *The Less Deceived* and not look out of place. The later poems of *The Less Deceived* were, after all, written very close in time to the earlier ones of *The Whitsun Weddings*, even though their appearance in book form was separated by nine years. Moreover, Larkin himself has warned off critics looking for 'development' in the sense of radical change, quoting Wilde's aphorism with approval: 'Only mediocrities develop'. In a conversation with Ian Hamilton, he defined the extent of his development as far as he could see it:

> I suppose I'm less likely to write a really bad poem now, but possibly equally less likely to write a really good

> one. If you can call that development, then I've
> developed.[2]

Larkin's assessment is accurate, though he is unduly modest about his present ability to write 'really good' poems. There are changes in *The Whitsun Weddings*: not departures from the themes and techniques of *The Less Deceived*, but modifications and improvements.

The Whitsun Weddings showed that Larkin had extended the range of his language. Characteristically, he did not extend it into some more or less esoteric area, as Auden did, say, in his use of psychoanalytical terms: Larkin reached downwards, making his language even more recognisably a version of the language as it is spoken. He uses the coarse colloquial in several poems. In 'A Study of Reading Habits', the final exclamation, 'Get stewed/ Books are a load of crap', is not a plea for universal philistinism, but a comment on the way reading loses its straightforward, easy emotional satisfactions as we grow older and no longer find it easy to make the obvious identifications we might have made with fictional characters in youth. The speaker reflects how he identified himself with the hero when a child, the villain when an adolescent; but in the final stanza, he refers to his maturity:

> Don't read much now: the dude
> Who lets the girl down before
> The hero arrives, the chap
> Who's yellow and keeps the store,
> Seem far too familiar.[3]

D. J. Enright condemns usages of the 'Books are a load of crap' variety, considering them epithets written 'clottishly'. Even such a great admirer of Larkin as Anthony Thwaite resents what he calls such 'manly nudging'. They miss the point, as John Press did with regard to the speaker in 'Church Going'. These comments give information about the speaker, not the books. In his maturity, he can see that he is neither hero nor villain, but just one of the minor characters who is a little despicable. The undependable dude and the cowardly store-keeper are 'far too familiar' because

2. 'Four Conversations', p. 77.
3. *T.W.W.*, p. 31.

the speaker realises that they are the characters he most resembles. His response is an act of bravado, a cliché designed to shield himself from his own uncomfortable perceptions, which shows the hollowness of the sentiment he is expressing.

Larkin develops his use of other 'ready-made' language. The colours of girls' dresses in 'The Whitsun Weddings' are 'lemons, mauves and olive-ochres'. This is not so much an eye for colour as a way of socially placing the girls, for these colour names, like the 'Lemon, sapphire, moss-green, rose' of the unreal women's nightclothes in 'The Large Cool Store', are the colour-names used by department stores to glamorise their products. Paradoxically, the mass-advertiser's word has a greater range and precision, in this context, than a word that the poet might have chosen to pinpoint his own discrimination of colour.

There seems to be more turning outward in the poems of *The Whitsun Weddings*, continuing the trend Larkin had started after the publication of *The North Ship*. He relies much more on the objective detail of an event or scene to evoke in his reader the sort of emotion that he experienced himself. In 'Home Is So Sad' he merely points to objects to illustrate the way in which a home seems to decline when people leave it, perhaps when one of the partners of a marriage dies, as if the things themselves pine away through having no one to please:

> You can see how it was:
> Look at the pictures and the cutlery.
> The music in the piano stool. That vase.[4]

These objective details tend to be more everyday than in the earlier volume. Images are chosen from the ordinary, and the ordinary is used to embody the poet's convictions. Odeons and cooling towers—the landscape of 'The Whitsun Weddings'—are even more familiar to us than horses at grass. Household effects are more likely to be 'that vase', of 'Home Is So Sad', or the 'toasters, washers, driers' of 'Here', than the 'books, china', of the earlier 'Poetry of Departures'.

There are more poems about other people in *The Whitsun Weddings*. Larkin exhibits his compassion for people quite different

4. *T.W.W.*, p. 17.

from himself: the desolate moustached women in 'Faith Healing', the disappointed widow in 'Love Songs in Age', 'the boy puking his heart out in the Gents', in 'Essential Beauty', the collection of misfits who inhabit public parks on weekday afternoons in 'Toads Revisited'.

Of course, there is an obverse to this coin, in that there are poems in *The Whitsun Weddings* that turn outwards the irony Larkin had earlier directed chiefly at himself. 'Naturally the Foundation Will Bear Your Expenses' is, I suppose, the sort of poem Ian Hamilton condemned as 'rollicking Betjemanesque' in his review of the collection for the *London Magazine*. Betjeman is very good at this kind of stinging verse, but the pejorative note of 'rollicking' is misplaced. The poem has a serious intent: Larkin has said himself that 'it's as serious as anything I have written.'[5] The fact that it is humorous does not make it trivial: Larkin has commended Betjeman for his ability to be funny and serious at the same time. The object of the satire is an ambitious and un-scrupulous academic, travelling from England to Bombay to repeat a lecture that he has already given at Berkeley, the Ameri-can university. He intends to repeat it on the B.B.C. Third Pro-gramme (as it then was) and finally turn it into a book, which he will publish with Chatto and Windus.

Aboard his plane, the academic's reflections show the serious nature of the poem.

> Crowds, colourless and careworn,
>   Had made my taxi late,
> Yet not till I was airborne
>   Did I recall the date—
> That day when Queen and Minister
>   And Band of Guards and all
> Still act their solemn-sinister
>   Wreath-rubbish in Whitehall.[6]

This individual's attitude contrasts sharply with Larkin's own. In 'Here' he shows a deeply-felt compassion for a 'cut-price crowd', children of a cheap and plastic age, a compassion expres-

5. Ian Hamilton, 'Four Conversations', p. 76.
6. *T.W.W.*, p. 13.

sed without a trace of being patronising. But the speaker of 'Naturally the Foundation Will Bear Your Expenses' feels no such compassion; rather, he is annoyed by the crowd because it held up his taxi. His dismissive attitude extends to another, larger crowd: the crowd killed in the two World Wars. Larkin has said that he listens to the radio broadcasts of the memorial service from the Cenotaph whenever he can, and he has expressed his feelings about the dead in 'MCMXIV', a moving poem describing a queue of people waiting to enlist in 1914, who are soon to be 'changed utterly' by the war.

In his work taken as a whole Larkin sees life as a bleak, sometimes horrifying business. 'Mr Bleaney' shows how mean life can be: Bleaney's very name combines the notions 'bleak' and 'mean' and ends in a diminutive, '-ey'. The poem is spoken by a man who moves into a furnished room recently vacated by Bleaney. He cannot help thinking that he is like his predecessor in many respects: surely a man's surroundings tell us something about what he is, and these surroundings are miserable and inadequate. He observes with nice detail and selectiveness:

> Flowered curtains, thin and frayed,
> Fall to within five inches of the sill,
>
> Whose window shows a strip of building land,
> Tussocky, littered. 'Mr Bleaney took
> My bit of garden properly in hand.'
> Bed, upright chair, sixty-watt bulb, no hook
>
> Behind the door, no room for books or bags—[7]

The speaker finds himself doing just what Bleaney must have done: 'I lie/Where Mr Bleaney lay, and stub my fags/On the same saucer-souvenir'; but Bleaney was less likely to wonder, as he does, whether the meanness of his surroundings could really tell us everything about him. The difference between the two men is that the speaker is an intellectual, and Bleaney was not. The speaker looks for bookshelves, but finds none: Bleaney had no need of them. Thinking too hard on his surroundings, the speaker is less equipped to cope with life than Bleaney is.

7. *T.W.W.*, p. 10.

Bleaney seems completely passive; so passive that his life is like a death-in-life: the landlady comments that Mr Bleaney had lived in her house until 'they moved him'. 'They' are his employers, but his landlady's choice of phrase makes it sound as if Bleaney was removed by undertakers, and this impression is reinforced when the speaker calls his room, near the end of the poem, a 'hired box'. But in fact, Bleaney is less passive than the speaker: at least Bleaney made himself comfortable, taught the landlady his preferences, managed to get her to buy a television set, did a bit of gardening. He had his 'yearly frame' worked out:

> the Frinton folk
> Who put him up for summer holidays,
> And Christmas at his sister's house in Stoke.

(This reference to Frinton is one of Larkin's rare slips, I think. Surely Frinton is a little too genteel for Bleaney? Stoke is more appropriate. Perhaps Larkin was attracted by the thin, flinty sound of its name.)

Lacking the speaker's sensitivity, Bleaney was fortunate: as Larkin said in 'Born Yesterday', happiness seems to consist in being 'dull'. The speaker is a man who thinks about his experience and finds patterns in it—writes poems about it. The contrast between Bleaney and his successor is illustrated in 'Nothing To Be Said', where Larkin observes the logical fact that, whoever you are, as soon as you are born, you continuously near death:

> Hours giving evidence
> Or birth, advance
> On death equally slowly.
> And saying so to some
> Means nothing; others it leaves
> Nothing to be said.[8]

Bleaney is one of those to whom it 'means nothing'; the speaker of 'Mr Bleaney' is one of the others. For a man like him there is 'Nothing to be said'; but ironically, there is also a poem, 'Nothing To Be Said'.

8. *T.W.W.*, p. 11.

In 'Mr Bleaney' life is poor and shoddy. Larkin has said that 'experience makes literature look insignificant beside life, as indeed life does beside death'. 'Ambulances' is informed by this conviction. The arrival of an ambulance is the irruption of the unexpected and inexplicable into life. Larkin's ambulances are grey and neutral and mysterious: like a man wearing dark glasses, they disconcertingly return 'none of the glances they absorb'. In the first stanza of the poem, the disturbing nature of the ambulances is suggested by the slightly discordant partial rhymes of 'thread/visited' and 'absorb/kerb'. Nobody is free from the threat: 'All streets in time are visited.' 'Visited' has overtones of demonic possession or plague rather than help or relief.

The arrival of the ambulance distresses those who see it as well as the invalid. Seeing the patient put into the ambulance, 'stowed', like so much inanimate cargo, the watchers

> sense the solving emptiness
> That lies just under all we do,
> And for a second get it whole,
> So permanent and blank and true.
> The fastened doors recede. *Poor soul*,
> They whisper at their own distress;[9]

In this context, the cliché '*Poor soul*' is charged with ironic meaning. If death is 'permanent and blank' 'emptiness', the very idea of a soul is out of place. It is a '*Poor soul*' because it doesn't exist.

The prospect of imminent, and immanent, death, as Dr Johnson said of the prospect of hanging within a fortnight, concentrates the mind wonderfully; though here, Larkin has no such grim humour:

> Far
> From the exchange of love to lie
> Unreachable inside a room
> The traffic parts to let go by
> Brings closer what is left to come,
> And dulls to distance all we are.

9. *T.W.W.*, p. 33.

'Ambulances' employs almost no similes or metaphors. The vehicles are 'closed like confessionals', and death is described as a 'solving emptiness'; but these are the only examples of figurative language in the poem. The statement is lucid and unencumbered: death seems to defy figurative expressions to come to terms with it, as if no manipulation of language can have more impact than the fact itself. Similarly, in 'Dockery and Son', death is 'the only end of age'. Again, no metaphor is needed, for the simple words, almost all monosyllables, have more impact.

Larkin never offers to explain why life is shaped for us, whether it is by death, as in 'Ambulances', or by our 'nature', over which we have little control, as in 'Mr Bleaney'. In fact, some poems reflect explicitly on how little we know about these things. In 'Dockery and Son' he explores the puzzlement that comes of wondering just why our lives come to be as they are, and why one man's life, though it starts very similarly, may end quite differently from another's.

'Dockery and Son' is the reminiscence of the poet on his journey home, having visited his old college. He has heard from the Dean that the son of one of his near contemporaries is up at the university now. His feeling of being somehow outside life, suggested in the pun on 'Death-suited', arises partly from this news, but it also seems as if the college itself excludes him, though it has admitted Dockery's representative:

> I try the door of where I used to live:
>
> Locked. The lawn spreads dazzlingly wide.
> A known bell chimes. I catch my train, ignored.[10]

The poem's strength is the same strength Larkin had shown in 'Church Going', and which he shows in so many of his poems: it makes the workings of the speaker's mind plausible and real, and is in this sense dramatic. Dockery has had a son, where the poet has had nothing; but the difference between the two men is not owing to Dockery's youthful decisiveness, but to each man's innate disposition to act in a certain way. Though the source of this perception is not openly stated, it seems to arise from the

10. *T.W.W.*, p. 37.

speaker's observations of the railway lines. At Sheffield he changed trains

> And ate an awful pie, and walked along
> The platform to its end to see the ranged
> Joining and parting lines reflect a strong
>
> Unhindered moon.

The railway lines, joining and parting, make a diagram of the respective careers of Dockery and the poet. They joined, briefly, at the university, and since then they have continuously diverged. The lines are set; they cannot decide to rejoin—to adapt slightly the words from later in the poem, they do what 'something hidden from them chose'. The fixed lines contrast with the moon, always in Larkin's poems a symbol of the untrammelled: in 'The Dancer', from *The North Ship*, the moon is 'anchorless'; in the recent 'Sad Steps', it is 'High and preposterous and separate', and as such 'a reminder of the strength and pain/Of being young.'

The spacious eight-line stanzas and straightforward ababcdcd rhyme scheme allow Larkin to make frequent modifications in tone, showing how the mind continually checks and tacks as it moves towards a conclusion.

> Dockery, now:
> Only nineteen, he must have taken stock
> Of what he wanted, and been capable
> Of . . . No, that's not the difference: rather, how
>
> Convinced he was he should be added to![11]

From this point on, the tone is surer, and the poem moves steadily towards the bald declaration in the fifth line of the last stanza. The hard bleakness of the statement is emphasised by Larkin's completely breaking with the iambic pentameter, which is the norm of the other lines. It is as if all theorising founders on this rock:

> Life is first boredom, then fear.
> Whether or not we use it, it goes,

11. *T.W.W.*, pp. 37–8.

PHILIP LARKIN

> And leaves what something hidden from us chose,
> And age, and then the only end of age.[12]

These lines seem to support Colin Falck, who said in a review of *The Whitsun Weddings* that Larkin misrepresents life, in the sense that he implies that life is pointless. 'Futile though life may be for the majority of people in our present society', Falck says, 'it is not futile in principle in the way that Larkin makes it seem.'[13] It is often alleged that Larkin's views are 'negative'. Ian Hamilton, who in other respects admires Larkin (as Colin Falck does), suggested that the great drawback to Larkin's work is its 'rather narrow range of negative attitudes'.[14]

Falck is saying that Larkin offers us a set of premises about life, and from them draws the conclusion that life is futile. No one would argue that, on the whole, Larkin's view of life is not grim; the events and objects that move him to write poems are generally those that reflect life's miserable aspects. But we could not, I think, fault him on the accuracy of what he does present—his premises are correct.

Falck considers that Larkin makes life seem futile, presumably by the expression of those 'negative attitudes' to which Hamilton refers. There is certainly an element in his work that suggests that he would like to be out of life altogether. 'Beneath it all,' he says in one poem, 'desire of oblivion runs.'[15] In 'Ambulances', death is called a 'solving emptiness'; and the question 'Where can we live but days?' is answered with an oddly lyrical yearning:

> Ah, solving that question
> Brings the priest and the doctor
> In their long coats
> Running over the fields.[16]

In 'Age' the speaker calls 'silence and space' 'dear translucent bergs'; but in other poems the desirability of nothingness is

12. *T.W.W.*, p. 38.
13. Colin Falck, '*The Whitsun Weddings*', *The Review*, XIV (December 1964), p. 5.
14. 'Poetry', *London Magazine*, p. 70.
15. 'Wants', *T.L.D.*, p. 22.
16. 'Days', *T.W.W.*, p. 27.

expressed in terms of an image of sea and sky. This is the case in 'Absences', where the panorama of sea and sky provokes an excited exclamation: 'Such attics cleared of me! Such absences!' In 'Here' the speaker says that the only place where 'unfenced existence' is possible is in the 'bluish neutral distance', where the land ends in sea and sky. Perhaps it reaches its most explicit statement in 'High Windows', published since *The Whitsun Weddings*. It is a poem about the way successive generations dispense with the taboos of their predecessors. But Larkin implies that real freedom has nothing to do with the lifting of social restraints:

> Rather than words comes the thought of high windows:
> The sun-comprehending glass,
> And beyond it, the deep blue air, that shows
> Nothing, and is nowhere, and is endless.[17]

Such yearning is a yearning for freedom, however, not necessarily a wish to be outside life because living is unbearable. Though Larkin is exhilarated by the idea, his attitude is not negative in the sense that he sees such a state of 'unfenced existence' as a sort of ideal condition, against which life may be matched and found wanting.

Larkin rejects any such ideal, not just because he is a prag-matist, but because there is a sense in which life's shortcomings, and our own, are to be preferred to any ideal. Larkin, like Hardy, sees that which makes us suffer in life not as a flaw, but as the means by which we achieve spiritual stature. In 'Essential Beauty' the ideal is described derogatorily as 'Pure crust, pure foam,/ Pure coldness', a surface with no warmth. The tone of the following lines contrasts strongly, showing that Larkin values living human imperfection above dead ideals. He speaks of

> our live imperfect eyes
> That stare beyond this world, where nothing's made
> As new or washed quite clean,[18]

17. Philip Larkin, 'High Windows', in *Word in the Desert: the Critical Quarterly Tenth Anniversary Number*, ed. C. B. Cox and A. E. Dyson, London 1968, p. 55.
18. *T.W.W.*, p. 42.

Some of Larkin's poems are, moreover, explicitly affirmative. 'Wedding Wind' has the cadences of a joyous psalm:

> Can even death dry up
> These new delighted lakes, conclude
> Our kneeling as cattle by all-generous waters?[19]

In 'The Whitsun Weddings', young newly-wed couples travelling in a train towards London will be like rain to the city, its postal districts 'packed like squares of wheat'. For the lambs born into the 'wretched width of cold' in 'First Sight' there is spring in store, 'Earth's immeasurable surprise'. 'First Sight' has indeed an easiness that makes it sound a little sentimental, with its rather pat rhymes, and the too-regular thump of the trochaic metre in the first stanza. However, it is difficult not to sound sentimental about lambs, and these defects are rare in Larkin's work. The poem does provide further evidence, though, that Larkin does not portray life as uniformly dull. That he finds it valuable is made clear by 'Church Going'.

'Dockery and Son', 'Mr Bleaney' and 'Ambulances' are different reactions to what is bleakest in life: the confrontation with what seems most intractable, whether it be death, or the 'innate assumptions', the 'style' that seems to have determined the way we live, resulting in Bleaney's shoddy room and, in 'Dockery and Son', the speaker's 'nothing'. The speaker in 'Mr Bleaney' feels 'dread' when he considers that 'How we live measures our own nature'; in 'Dockery and Son' the emotion following on a similar apprehension is numbness; in 'Ambulances' there is horror at a vicarious confrontation with death. But more often, Larkin's poems suggest, our feeling about life is less traumatic. Martin Dodsworth believes that Larkin's poems deal not with suffering, but with 'sadness, a great damp patch in our lives.'[20] This blanket statement however tends to diminish the intensity of feeling in some poems: besides those mentioned above, 'Send No Money' is harsh and bitter, not 'sad', and 'sadness' is really an inexact word for the emotion in 'MCMXIV'.

19. *T.L.D.*, p. 15.
20. Martin Dodsworth, 'The Climate of Pain in Recent Poetry', *London Magazine*, IV (November 1964), p. 89.

An important group of poems where this is true in *The Whitsun Weddings* is the love poems; or, if that term is misleading (at least one commentator has said that there are no love poems in this collection)[21] we should say, the poems about love. Larkin confesses on the L.P. record of his reading of the poems: ' "Broadcast" is about as near as I get in this collection to a love poem. Not, I am afraid, very near.' This is true: 'Broadcast' is more about infatuation than love. The poet listens to a radio broadcast of a concert he knows the loved one to be attending. Small details individualise her in his description: he seems to pick out imperfections, making a rather bitchy reference to her insensitivity about her clothing, in an attempt to persuade himself that his emotion is absurdly in excess of its object.

> One of your gloves unnoticed on the floor
> Beside those new, slightly-outmoded shoes.[22]

He cannot sustain his mental picture of her, however. The real world, a world of decay and diminution, forces itself in upon him:

> Here it goes quickly dark. I lose
> All but the outline of the still and withering
>
> Leaves on half-emptied trees.

At the end of the broadcast he vainly tries to catch her individual sound amongst the applause of the rest of the audience. His vocabulary indicates the judgement of his reason on the irrational, childish emotion: he is contemptuous of himself. The chords of the orchestra 'overpower' his mind 'All the more shamelessly' 'by being distant': sentimentally, we always yearn more for what is unreachable, whether through time or space. He is 'desperate'

> to pick out
> Your hands, tiny in all that air, applauding.

The word again shows an emotional over-reaction.

In 'Broadcast' it seems that the poet's thoughts about the

21. J. L. Featherstone, 'Poetry of Commonplaces', *New Republic*, 6 March 1965, p. 28.
22. *T.W.W.*, p. 14.

woman only emphasise his own loneliness. Love does not cure loneliness and melancholy, but compounds it. Similarly, in 'Love Songs in Age', a woman who in her widowhood finds old copies of love songs she would play when she was young is distressed by her knowledge of their emptiness, and of the inability of love to do all we claim for it. The songs evoke our common conception of love, but in her maturity, the woman knows its true limitations:

> The glare of that much-mentioned brilliance, love,
>   Broke out, to show
> Its bright incipience sailing above,
> Still promising to solve, and satisfy,
> And set unchangeably in order. So
>   To pile them back, to cry,
> Was hard, without lamely admitting how
> It had not done so then, and could not now.[23]

Here, love makes an empty promise to 'solve'; but in 'Ambulances' death is the only thing that offers solutions: it is the 'solving emptiness'. It seems that nothing can cure our ills while we are alive. In *Endgame*, Beckett's Hamm yells, 'You're on earth, there's no cure for that'. It may be that these two very different artists are here in agreement, though Larkin would not make so emphatic a statement (nor would Beckett in his own person, of course; Hamm's name implies his over-dramatic delivery) and he certainly would not follow the nihilism of Beckett's recent work.

The trouble with love, Larkin suggests, is not that it doesn't exist, but that when we find it, it doesn't match up to the idea we had of it, nor does it do all we expected of it. He says in one poem, 'Talking in Bed', that two people in bed ought to have all defences down, and be able to talk most freely and openly. But in fact:

> At this unique distance from isolation
>
> It becomes still more difficult to find
> Words at once true and kind,
> Or not untrue and not unkind.[24]

23. *T.W.W.*, p. 12.
24. *T.W.W.*, p. 29.

The guarded negatives of the last line indicate the defensive tone the speaker feels he must adopt towards the person who shares his bed: a careful concern not to hurt, but not to lie.

'Talking in Bed' illustrates Larkin's great talent for ending his poems memorably. His endings are memorable not necessarily because they are resounding or aphoristic—though Larkin can end resoundingly (as in 'Church Going') or with an aphorism ('Nothing, like something, happens anywhere')—but because they catch the mood of the poem as a whole in a few words:

> Never such innocence again.
>   ('MCMXIV')
>   . . . the trite untransferable
> Truss-advertisement, truth.
>   ('Send No Money')
> And age, and then the only end of age.
>   ('Dockery and Son')

The list could be multiplied.

The poem also shows Larkin's technical mastery of the iambic pentameter. The lines in 'Talking in Bed' are all recognisably iambic pentameters, with the exception of the last and next last, an iambic tetrameter and an iambic trimeter respectively. Almost all the lines have the standard ten syllables, but there is no one line that is completely regular. The impression of some-one speaking, or rather thinking, is achieved through subtle modifications in rhythm, and maintained throughout. It is not that Larkin has written in an irregular metre, but that he has taken full advantage of the almost infinite variations possible to the English iambic line in terms of substitution and reversal of feet.

The poem that best defines Larkin's attitude towards love, 'An Arundel Tomb' is, for me, his greatest success. The starting point of the poem is the monumental sculpture of a pair of stone figures, man and wife, lying side by side over a tomb. The tomb in question, incidentally, is not at Arundel: it is a tomb belonging to the Howard family, once Earls and Countesses of Arundel, now Dukes and Duchesses of Norfolk, in Chichester Cathedral. This tomb is differentiated from most monumental sculpture of a similar kind because the stone figures are holding hands, and this affects the poet profoundly.

'An Arundel Tomb' might be an ironic rejoinder to Marvell's *carpe diem*, 'To His Coy Mistress'. Though Marvell says, 'The grave's a fine and private place,/Though none, I think, do there embrace', Larkin's Earl and Countess *do* embrace in the tomb, or so the sculpture would have us believe. But it may be that the endurance of this stone embrace implies more fortitude in their love than it really possessed. Their 'attitude' was 'hardly meant', just 'Thrown off in helping to prolong/The Latin names around the base'. In the first and third stanzas there is an uninsistent pun on the verb in 'lie in stone' and 'They would not think to lie so long'. But what touches the speaker most is that their 'attitude' has remained. Here, Larkin again capitalises on a double meaning. Their 'attitude'—the pose of the stone figures—has lasted through the centuries, but so has their 'attitude'—the cast of mind that suggested the pose to the Earl and his wife.

With superb economy, Larkin indicates the passage of the years; the time of the Earl and Countess has passed into vagueness:

> Snow fell, undated. Light
> Each summer thronged the glass. A bright
> Litter of birdcalls strewed the same
> Bone-riddled ground. And up the paths
> The endless altered people came,[25]

The last line of this stanza is one of Larkin's very rare completely regular iambic lines, where heavy stresses of equal weight alternate with light ones, again of equal weight. Here, its steady thump is like a clock's, regularly tocking the time away, suggesting the continuous stream of 'altered people', corpses and visitors, coming to the graveyard.

But the impulse in people to make gestures like the Earl's and Countess's, an impulse basic enough to be called an 'almost instinct', has not altered. This is constant in people, however appearances may change. The 'attitude' of the Earl and Countess has persisted in the 'altered people'.

25. *T.W.W.*, p. 45.

Now, helpless in the hollow of
An unarmorial age, a trough
Of smoke in slow suspended skeins
Above their scrap of history,
Only an attitude remains:

Time has transfigured them into
Untruth. The stone fidelity
They hardly meant has come to be
Their final blazon, and to prove
Our almost-instinct almost true:
What will survive of us is love.[26]

The 'almost-instinct' may be misguided, but it is valuable and affecting as an enduring feature of human relationships. The Earl and Countess end on a fine and touching gesture that is less true than the lasting stone embrace makes us think; similarly, 'An Arundel Tomb' contrives to end on a fine and memorable line that the poet warns us is only 'almost true', an 'untruth'.

'Untruth' is a carefully chosen word, a word 'not untrue and not unkind' such as the speaker sought in 'Talking in Bed', which has not the harshness of its synonyms, 'lie' or 'falsehood'. The repetition of 'almost', making the sense of the sentence slightly hard to follow, also blunts the cutting edges of the fact. These things hint at Larkin's regret in having to admit that the gesture of the stone figures, and our reciprocal gesture of accepting it at its face value, is less than true. Larkin insists on truth gently: he is charitable towards our false beliefs. This unsentimental charity is his most valuable quality, I believe. He has said:

> Separating the man who suffers from the man who
> creates is all right—we separate the petrol from the
> engine—but the dependence of the second on the first
> is complete.[27]

One admires Larkin as a man who feels as well as a poet who creates, and is glad that the two are not separate in him. Part of the strength of 'An Arundel Tomb' derives from the unwillingness of

26. *T.W.W.*, p. 46.
27. Philip Larkin, 'Context', *London Magazine*, I (February 1962), p. 32.

the poet himself to criticise human weakness from the outside. The reader knows that Larkin shares the human failings he recognises in the poem; his choosing to end the poem on that line, and the gentleness of his insistence on truth, derive from the same impulse that urges us to accept that 'What will survive of us is love'.

The disappointment almost inevitably attendant upon love is caused not by anything inherent in love itself, but by our beliefs about it: our mistaken conviction that 'What will survive of us is love', or that love will 'solve, and satisfy, and set unchangeably in order'. In one of the several perceptive articles he has written on Hardy's work, Larkin comments on the fact that Hardy's greatest love poetry was written for his first wife, in regret and remorse after her death:

> This kind of paradox is inseparable from poetic creation,
> and indeed from life altogether. At times it almost
> appears a sort of basic insincerity in human affection.
> At others it seems a flaw built deeply into the working
> of the emotions, creating an inevitable bias in life
> towards unhappiness.[28]

It is important to notice that Larkin closely associates this 'flaw' with the writing of poetry. In 'Send No Money' in particular, the suffering attendant upon learning truth through experience turns a naïve young man into a poet. Hardy's great love poems arise directly out of his knowledge of what his love and marriage were like in practice, and his parallel apprehension of what they might have been like, given the way they started. As Larkin himself has said on a different matter: 'Things begin bright but end dully. If you couldn't imagine things much better than they are, it wouldn't be half so bad.'[29] And this is the 'flaw' Larkin mentions: the 'almost-instinct' to imagine things much better than they are, in love and in life generally.

This tendency is the subject-matter of several of Larkin's poems, and his appreciation of it underlies many more. Larkin examines two of its aspects in particular. One is directly linked

28. Philip Larkin, 'Mrs Hardy's Memories', *Critical Quarterly*, IV (Spring 1962), p. 79.
29. John Horder, 'Poet on the 8.15', p. 9.

to what he says about Hardy; the other is more basic: he reflects directly on the status of our idealisations. In the first, we know the truth through experience, and contrast it with what might have been; in the second, the glare of idealisation blinds us to present truth.

'Reference Back' explicitly states the paradox Larkin noted with regard to Hardy. The speaker is a man in his thirties visiting his parents' home. Mother and son have little in common, he realises: their relationship is summed up in the grating word reiterated throughout the poem, 'unsatisfactory'. But a sudden contact is made between them when he plays a jazz record his mother overhears. She calls, '*That was a pretty one*'. Looking for a word 'not untrue and not unkind', the mother makes a lame and inappropriate comment, but at least it makes some sort of bridge between herself and her son. However, the bridge only serves to emphasise the gap. At once he sees their relationship as it was, and as it is, with all its promise unfulfilled:

> Truly, though our element is time,
> We are not suited to the long perspectives
> Open at each instant of our lives.
> They link us to our losses: worse,
> They show us what we have as it once was,
> Blindingly undiminished, just as though
> By acting differently we could have kept it so.[30]

The trouble is not that we have ruined what might have been different—the last line indicates that however we might have acted, life would have turned out the same—but that it seems to us in retrospect that we might have achieved something better had we acted differently. The formal characteristics of the poem emphasise the awkwardness, which is all the speaker is left with. It is very loosely constructed, lines varying in length, stanzas varying in size. The rhyme units, couplets, are the smallest possible, and so do not draw the poem together as larger units would have done. In one case, even the couplet is divided by a stanza break. We are further disconcerted by the irregular pattern of partial-, half- and full-rhymes.

30. *T.W.W.*, p. 40.

PHILIP LARKIN

Where 'Reference Back' is spoken by a son, we might read 'Home Is So Sad' as an expression of his mother's emotions when she looks at her home after her son has left it. In an interview with a *Times* correspondent, Larkin said that such a mother once wrote to him, having read 'Home Is So Sad' in a magazine. 'She wrote to say her children had grown up and gone,' Larkin recalled, 'and she felt precisely this emotion I was trying to express in the poem.'[31] Empty, the home can no longer look or feel as it did when full. It is 'A joyous shot at how things ought to be/ Long fallen wide'. The metaphor of the arrow is reminiscent of the closing lines of 'The Whitsun Weddings', where the 'sense of falling' in a braking train full of newly-married young people, presumably just about to establish homes, is like that of an 'arrow shower'. The couples themselves are a 'joyous shot', but perhaps their homes too will decline, the arrow fall wide.

The title of 'MCMXIV', which explores another of these 'perspectives', suggests a monument to those killed in the Great War. The poem describes England as it must have been when just on the brink of the fighting—in a state of 'innocence', unaware of the bloody mess that the 'war to end wars' was to become. Men were lining up to volunteer, their ideals still intact. Larkin describes the physical details those of us too young to have been present must know from jerky old newsreels and sepia photographs. The poem has no main verb, and though Larkin has disclaimed any intention in this, saying that it was a complete accident, it is entirely appropriate that no action is indicated: it is as if the time were frozen:

> Those long uneven lines
> Standing as patiently
> As if they were stretched outside
> The Oval or Villa Park,
> The crowns of hats, the sun
> On moustached archaic faces
> Grinning as if it were all
> An August Bank Holiday lark;[32]

31. 'Speaking of Writing XIII: Philip Larkin', p. 16.
32. *T.W.W.*, p. 28.

The men are caught on the edge of knowledge; only we, with our knowledge of their future, know that they will soon lose their 'innocence'. The melancholy of the speaker is caught by the single, fleeting rhyme in the fifth and ninth lines of each stanza; but the poem affects us chiefly through the tension between what is said and what is left unsaid. We have the knowledge the men are about to attain, the knowledge of millions of dead which 'MCMXIV' recalls. It is the simultaneous apprehension of reality and their false ideal which moves us.

In the group of poems I have been discussing above, Larkin opposes our conception of things as they are to that of things as they promised to be. In another group he opposes things as they are to things as we imagine them to be. The title of 'Essential Beauty' ironically contrasts the Platonic essence with the contemporary equivalent, the advertisement hoarding. Of course, there is a radical difference between Plato's view and Larkin's. Plato's world of 'Essential Beauty' is the 'real' one, in his system, and the world of imperfections and inconsistences in which we live is illusory. For Larkin, our world is 'real', 'where nothing's made/As new or washed quite clean'. Larkin gives a factual description of what is represented on a selection of these hoardings. We normally accept the conventions of the advertisement-world: giant glasses of milk, chairs drawn up before cups as if before a fire, and so on; but their being presented to us in a different medium, words rather than pictures, makes them surreal. This effect is increased by the juxtapositions Larkin makes between objects from the real world and those from the advertisements, which 'Screen graves with custard, cover slums with praise/Of motor-oil and cuts of salmon'. The elliptical language suggests that custard really is poured on graves, cuts of salmon laid over slums. The salmon and the custard obscure the realities. The main verb of the sentence that opens the poem is delayed till the end of the fourth line. We are given the surreal description with almost no indication that these strange things are, in fact, merely advertisement-hoardings, which stand between us and disturbing reality. Only 'frames' in the first line offers a clue.

Larkin does not take the conventional view of advertisements. He has said that as a young man, he was like most other young intellectuals in regarding them as utterly meretricious. In his maturity, however, he sees them as rather pathetic. When we are gulled by advertisements, or by idealisations of any kind, we deserve sympathy and compassion, not ridicule. After all, to be fooled by an advertisement is a mistake only different in degree from that of the men in 'MCMXIV', who obviously deserve our sympathy.

It is paradoxical, perhaps, that in a poem concerned to point out that the ideal world is a delusion, Larkin should give it such lyrical expression. It is a world where

> dying smokers sense
> Walking towards them through some dappled park
> As if on water that unfocused she
> No match lit up, nor drag ever brought near,
> Who now stands newly clear,
> Smiling, and recognising, and going dark.[33]

The ideal is expressed with melancholy, not bitterness or satire. As in the final stanza of 'An Arundel Tomb', Larkin acknowledges that he suffers like the rest of humanity from the disease he diagnoses. He too sees the attraction of these delusions, and so does not despise others for them.

The reaction of 'Titch Thomas' in 'Sunny Prestatyn' to one of these hoardings is quite unlike Larkin's own. The hoarding in this poem depicts a pretty girl, 'the universal symbol of happiness', Larkin explains on his L.P. recording of *The Whitsun Weddings*. The hoarding advertises a seaside resort: the girl is dressed in a bathing costume and, somewhat hopefully, she kneels before a clump of palms. Her perfection could not last, for she was 'too good for this life':

> She was slapped up one day in March.
> A couple of weeks, and her face
> Was snaggle-toothed and boss-eyed;
> Huge tits and a fissured crotch
> Were scored well in, and the space
> Between her legs held scrawls

33. *T.W.W.*, p. 42.

That set her fairly astride
A tuberous cock and balls

Autographed *Titch Thomas*, while
Someone had used a knife
Or something to stab right through
The moustached lips of her smile.[34]

This is another example of Larkin's use of the coarse colloquial
for a particular effect. Here, it is appropriate to use words like
'cock', 'balls', 'tits' and so on for the scrawls on the poster—more
polite usages would have described the drawings less exactly,
and would have seemed silly and prim and inappropriate. These
words, being violent themselves, enact the violence of the desecra-
tion. But Titch Thomas's is an over-reaction: he behaves in this
way because of sexual frustration, as his name, and the fact that
it is signed on the 'cock and balls' indicates. The girl is a delusion,
an image of all that has been denied to him. The relationship
between reality and delusion is a common theme in modern
literature, but it is usually conceived in T. S. Eliot's terms:
'human kind/Cannot bear very much reality'. For Titch Thomas,
the opposite is true: he cannot bear very much delusion, for it is such
a violent reproach to the way he lives. He has to deface the poster.

Larkin's regretful insistence that our idealisations are delusions
is paralleled by his bitterness at the suffering inflicted by the truth,
though this bitterness is a creative force in his poems. I observed
above that in 'Mr Bleaney', the speaker probably suffered more
than Bleaney, because the latter was not reflective—or not a poet,
perhaps. Similarly, in 'Nothing To Be Said' the last line is
ambiguous: to be told the truth that life is a continuous approach
to death leaves, for those to whom the observation is meaningful,
'Nothing to be said'; but it also leaves the poem of the same name.
In 'Send No Money', the process of maturing of someone who
set out to find truth is described. The naïve cliché of the speaker
when young, 'All the other lads there/Were itching to have a
bash', suggests his innocence; and it contrasts sharply with the
resounding words of the middle-aged man, who has learnt his
truth through experience:

34. *T.W.W.*, p. 35.

> Half life is over now,
> And I meet full face on dark mornings
> The bestial visor, bent in
> By the blows of what happened to happen.[35]

The poem's force lies in the contrast between the first stanza and the last. Achieving maturity and truth has been painful, but it has turned the youth into a poet. These later lines provide a retrospective irony on the earlier ones. The alliteration of the 'b's suggests the bludgeoning force of what is called in the poem 'the hail/Of occurrence', which will always 'clobber life out'. In the light of this, the cliché 'have a bash' is given an unexpected wrench. The youth will literally 'have a bash', but he will receive it, rather than give it: he will suffer 'the blows of what happened to happen'. The pure stress metre of 'Send No Money' —used more often in *The Whitsun Weddings* than in *The Less Deceived*—allows great flexibility in individual lines, while keeping the unity of the poem. The lines in the last stanza have three stresses, but line twenty is dragged out to eleven syllables, where the opening lines have only six or seven:

> By the blóws of what háppened to háppen.

The regular, heavy stresses, the slowness and length of this line enact the steady, continual blows the speaker has suffered.

The end of the poem comments on the innocent eagerness of the youth, as it was reported in the first lines. The alliteration of the 't's and 's's suggest a spat bitterness:

> What does it prove? Sod all.
> In this way I spent youth,
> Tracing the trite untransferable
> Truss-advertisement, truth.

This observation is quite different from a rather more famous one on truth, which alliterates 't's with a contrasting effect: 'Beauty is truth, truth beauty'. But Larkin does not use the metaphor in the last line for its alliterative qualities alone. A truss may be

35. *T.W.W.*, p. 43.

restricting and objectionable, but its wearer is able to function better with it than without. Larkin's whole poetic output since *The North Ship* shows his persistent effort to face truth. Though he is sympathetic towards the delusions of others—'we are nudged from comfort', in the words of an earlier poem,[36] not bludgeoned with the truth—he does not ignore them.

The title poem of *The Whitsun Weddings* is like 'Church Going' in its positive affirmation. The speaker of the poem is a man taking a train journey from the North of England to London on a Whit Saturday. Each time he stops at a station, he sees a wedding-party, saying farewell to a newly married couple.

The poem may be fruitfully compared with John Betjeman's fine 'The Metropolitan Railway'. Betjeman's poem is a reminiscence that contrasts modern times with the days of 'Early Electric', its remains still to be seen where the speaker is sitting, in the station buffet at Baker Street. (At least, they were still to be seen when the poem was written. Now, alas, they are silent under soot and chrome.) There has been a decline since then, which may be seen in little in the lives of a young couple who were married when electric trains were new. The landscape has changed for the worse:

> An Odeon flashes fire
> Where stood their villa by the murmuring fir.[37]

When Pinner had 'leafy lanes', and the countryside started at Preston Road, the couple 'felt so sure on their electric trip/That Youth and Progress were in partnership'. But now the husband is dead, the wife dying:

> Cancer has killed him. Heart is killing her.

It seems that urban London has murdered him, creeping outwards, like the disease through his body, over the suburbs.

Larkin's poem, though similar in some surface respects, is concerned with what is enduring rather than what is decaying. Betjeman is profoundly moved by the false optimism of his young

36. 'Arrivals, Departures', *T.L.D.*, p. 44.
37. John Betjeman, *Collected Poems*. Enlarged edition, compiled and with an introduction by the Earl of Birkenhead, London 1970, p. 213.

Edwardian couple, but is cynical about what modernity has meant for them. Larkin does not suggest that *his* young married people are necessarily impoverished by the decay of their landscape, a landscape remarkably similar to Betjeman's:

> An Odeon went past, a cooling tower,

The younger poet sees that at every age, such marriages start with hopes appropriate to the times, and this very fact is worthy of celebration. Something is constant in life, even though the topography alters: we may remember the sentiment of 'An Arundel Tomb', that the 'attitude' exemplified by the Earl and Countess has not changed through the ages.

'The Whitsun Weddings' shows some of Larkin's talents to their greatest advantage. He finely evokes the sights and smells of the country. The description is not merely of what one sees, but of what he sees when he is moving: cars are blinding windscreens; greenhouses a sudden flash of reflected sunlight; hedges are green lines that rise and fall as he passes.

> All afternoon, through the tall heat that slept
> > For miles inland,
> A slow and stopping curve southwards we kept.
> Wide farms went by, short-shadowed cattle, and
> Canals with floatings of industrial froth;
> A hothouse flashed uniquely: hedges dipped
> And rose: and now and then a smell of grass
> Displaced the reek of buttoned carriage-cloth
> Until the next town, new and nondescript,
> Approached with acres of dismantled cars.[38]

The description is always carrying us onward, and we move through a landscape that gets progressively more southern: through the areas of heavy industry around Sheffield, through rural gaps between towns, to the car-manufacturing Midlands. By disrupting the iambic pentameter with the reversal of a foot immediately after the caesura, the third line enacts the stopping and starting of the train; and Larkin delays the main verb of the

38. *T.W.W.*, p. 21.

first sentence of the stanza until the end of the third line, so that it pulls us up short.

Larkin is one of the very few contemporary poets—Betjeman is another—who give us a clear picture of what the England they live in actually looks like. In neither poet's work, however, is topography often the central concern: it is usually the background to people's lives. Betjeman's Baker Street station buffet is lovingly described, as is the 'autumn-scented Middlesex' of the early years of this century. But Baker Street is important for reasons other than nostalgia for the Edwardian:

> Of all their loves and hopes on hurrying feet
> Thou art the worn memorial, Baker Street.

Larkin too is primarily concerned with people: those he sees from his train window are more important than the landscape against which they are seen: the wedding-parties are yet more closely observed than their background. The objective exactness of the description prevents his interest from seeming superior or sentimental:

> The fathers with broad belts under their suits
> And seamy foreheads; mothers loud and fat;
> An uncle shouting smut; and then the perms,
> The nylon gloves and jewellery-substitutes,
> The lemons, mauves, and olive-ochres that
>
> Marked off the girls unreally from the rest.[39]

For these girls, what happens is a 'religious wounding'. Even for the earthy fathers, the day has been a 'wholly farcical' success: we are surely meant to catch the suspicion of 'holy' in the adverb. For the mothers, it is 'like a happy funeral'. These figurative expressions express the importance, even the sacredness, of the marriage-days. The funeral is the mothers' own, for their sons and daughters are taking over the role of new creators that their parents have now abdicated.

This theme is amplified in 'Afternoons', which suggests that the

39. *T.W.W.*, p. 22.

lives of young suburban mothers decline, until they are little more than the sum of their routine tasks. The poem is set in that time of year when summer changes to autumn: metaphorically, the time of life of the mothers themselves. The leaves are being pushed into drifts by the wind; the mothers have as little control over their lives as the leaves over their movement.

> Their beauty has thickened.
> Something is pushing them
> To the side of their own lives.[40]

To equate the decline of the year with the fading of the mothers is to suggest that decay in human life is not something we can prevent. It is a natural process, generations succeeding each other in natural cycles. The mothers release their children on to the 'recreation ground', where, we are told, the mothers had their courting places, and the children are creating new ones. Larkin capitalises on both meanings of 'recreation'. The children are released not only to play, but to take up the new cycle of marriage and childbirth through which their mothers, like the mothers of 'The Whitsun Weddings', have passed.

'The Whitsun Weddings' ends joyfully. Anthony Thwaite once produced a radio programme that included a reading of the poem, and he wrote to Larkin for advice on how it should be performed. Larkin explained that it should hold a carefully sustained note until the very end, when it should 'lift off the ground'. The young couples will bring life to London: they are rain falling on the 'squares of wheat' that are the postal districts of the city:

> We slowed again,
> And as the tightened brakes took hold, there swelled
> A sense of falling, like an arrow-shower
> Sent out of sight, somewhere becoming rain.[41]

40. *T.W.W.*, p. 44.
41. *T.W.W.*, p. 23.

6   Uncollected Poems

It would be of little use for me to discuss the poems Larkin has published since *The Whitsun Weddings* in great detail, since they are not yet readily available, in the form of a collection, to the general reader. Some have appeared in national periodicals—the *New Statesman*, the *Listener*—but others in journals of a much more specialist interest, like the *Critical Quarterly*. However, I hope that at least I can show the directions Larkin's work has been taking since 1964.

He has continued to produce poems at his steady, slow rate. Talking to Ian Hamilton in the year in which *The Whitsun Weddings* was published, Larkin said that he hoped to improve, rather than change: 'I don't think I want to change; just to become better at what I am.'[1] He was fifty in 1972, and in a radio broadcast in honour of his birthday, he rather modified his attitude, expressing a hope that he *would* change: 'What I should like to do is write *different* kinds of poems, that might be by different people. Someone once said that the great thing is not to be different from other people, but to be different from yourself.' Larkin rather wryly justified his choosing to read 'The Explosion', a poem about a pit disaster, from his recent work: it 'isn't especially like me, or like what I fancy I'm supposed to be like'. Larkin had half made the point before, in 1962, in selecting a poem for *Poet's Choice*, an anthology of poems chosen by authors from their own work. He chose 'Absences': 'I fancy it sounds like a different, better poet rather than myself.'[2] In the course of my discussion of Larkin's work, I have tried to show that its range is far wider than his detractors often allow; and in fact, 'Absences' is not so unusual a poem when seen in the light of other pieces, like 'Age', 'Here', and, more recently, 'High Windows', a poem

1. 'Four Conversations', p. 77.
2. 'Absences', *Poet's Choice*, p. 202.

contributed to the tenth anniversary issue of the *Critical Quarterly* in 1968.

Larkin has certainly gone on to explore certain avenues he began to open up in *The Whitsun Weddings*. His only satirical pieces in that collection were 'Naturally the Foundation Will Bear Your Expenses', a lampoon of the attitudes of one kind of professional intellectual, and 'Take One Home For The Kiddies', a vicious thrust at those who treat animals as objects of trade. Since 1964, Larkin has published several satirical pieces: he is looking outward more and more in his poems, continuing a trend which seems to have become more marked in successive books.

In 'Annus Mirabilis' Larkin speaks as a man who envies the sexual freedom of the young, but who just missed their boat.

> Sexual intercourse began
> In nineteen sixty-three
> (Which was rather late for me)—
> Between the end of the *Chatterley* ban
> And the Beatles' first LP.[3]

In *No! In Thunder* the American critic Leslie Fiedler adapts a saying of Goethe's. Goethe advised, 'Be careful what you wished for in your youth, for you will get it in your middle age'. Fiedler considers his recasting of the aphorism to be more horrible still: 'Be careful what you wish for in your youth, for *the young* will get it in your middle age.' The speaker of 'Annus Mirabilis' would probably agree.

Larkin has taken another swing at the professional academic. In 'Posterity' he satirises the American junior college professor, who has to turn out his book or Ph.D. thesis in order to 'get tenure'. 'Jake Balokowsy' (the pun in his name shows Larkin's opinion of him) looks upon his work as a kind of literary manual labouring, done only to make a comfortable living. Jake has no sympathy with the subject of his biography, and even feels a little cheated that he is not a Rimbaud or a Dylan Thomas: nothing really nasty has happened in his life, which might have enlivened his tedious task.

3. 'Annus Mirabilis', *London Magazine*, IX (January 1970), p. 29.

'What's he like?
Christ, I just told you. Oh, you know the thing,
That crummy textbook stuff from Freshman Psych.,
Not out of kicks or something happening—
One of those old-type *natural* fouled-up guys.'[4]

'Posterity' is rather acid, but other poems are more straightforwardly humorous. 'The Cardplayers', is a verbal equivalent of
a Dutch genre painting. Just as in 'Essential Beauty', descriptions
of advertisement hoardings had thrown on them a light that
showed up their surreal quality, 'The Cardplayers', using the
same device of presenting the familiar in an unfamiliar medium,
makes us see these paintings in a new way, all their crudeness
obvious. Three men, 'Jan Van Hogspeuw', 'Dick Dogstoerd' and
'Old Prijck', are comfortable in a warm inn during a rainstorm.
They are a sort of basic humanity, hardly more than their natural
functions: Jan 'pisses at the dark', 'farts, gobs at the grate', and
Dick belches.

The form of the poem is closely akin to that of 'Absences':
description, followed by a one-line coda on the poem, which
contains two exclamations:

Rain, wind and fire! The secret, bestial peace![5]

The 'absences', which the poet envied in the earlier piece, were
sea and sky—water and air. These men are reduced to elements:
pissing, farting, gobbing, belching. The rain and wind are within
the inn as well as outside, in a sense. The poem suggests that the
only freedom possible in this world is a lapse into bestiality, for
these men with their absurd, punning names are certainly free
from any kind of social restraint, at least.

'Vers de Société' is probably the best of these satirical pieces.
Despite its title, it is not light verse in the sense of being
non-serious, though in parts it is bitchily funny. Here is
Larkin's adaptation of an invitation to a party he knows he will
hate:

4. 'Posterity', *New Statesman*, 28 June 1968, p. 876.
5. 'The Cardplayers', *Encounter*, XXXV (October 1970), p. 41.

PHILIP LARKIN

> *My wife and I have asked a crowd of craps*
> *To come and waste their time and ours : perhaps*
> *You'd care to join us?*[6]

But the poem is literally about society, and how difficult it is, for
many reasons, to avoid it as one ages. 'Vers de Société' has a great
variety and depth of emotion, from stinging slaps at others (like
that 'bitch/Who's read nothing but *Which*') to evocations of the
darkening autumn evening and the closing in of life. Even the
thrust at the 'bitch' is less uncharitable than it would appear, for
the poem makes it clear that such diatribes stem from the speaker's
feelings of failure rather than any conviction of his own superior-
ity. It is as much impotent bravado as 'Books are a load of crap',
from 'A Study of Reading Habits'. For the speaker, being alone
means facing his own questions about himself, for 'Beyond the
light stand failure and remorse'. The poem shows how constant
Larkin's themes have remained since 1946: disappointment in
life, the pressures of society on the individual, the desire to
escape those pressures together with the fear of the isolation such
escape brings, the encroachment of time.

Larkin has also begun to write poems that might be described
as 'public', dealing with specific contemporary events. He contributed a couplet on the student demonstrations at the London
School of Economics to a collection of essays on educational prob-
lems, *Black Paper II*, edited by C. B. Cox and A. E. Dyson. *Black
Paper II* took a conservative line on education, its contributors
considering many new educational trends to be regressive. In 1969,
Larkin published a poem in the *Sunday Times* deploring Britain's
increasing insularity, especially with regard to the withdrawal of
British troops from areas they had traditionally policed. This was
one of the effects of the great cuts in military expenditure made
in 1968 by the Labour Government then in power.

Robert Conquest, an old friend of Larkin's and, according to
George Macbeth, who introduced the radio broadcast in celebra-
tion of Larkin's fiftieth birthday, 'a fellow Conservative', said of
'Homage to a Government' that it 'looks back to the days of
Empire, whatever its faults, as a period of vision and scope, a
broader time for Britain; not merely physically, but also in that

6. 'Vers de Société', *New Statesman*, 18 June 1971, p. 854.

the motives and feelings involved were not petty and self-seeking, as against what he [Larkin] sees as a constricted, economically obsessed present'. The poem is a satire, but its tone shows that it is a satire conceived more in sorrow than in anger. Perhaps it is more an elegy, as the title suggests, but an elegy mourning the diminution of the integrity of the British. There will still be statues in the parks in future, relics of past national honour, but the 'attitude' (to borrow an apposite word from 'An Arundel Tomb') they represent will have vanished. Our children will inherit not a feeling of duty towards other countries less fortunate than their own, and pride in fulfilling that duty, but cash.

> Next year we shall be living in a country
> That brought its soldiers home for lack of money.
> The statues will be standing in the same
> Tree-muffled squares, and look nearly the same.
> Our children will not know it's a different country.
> All we can hope to leave them now is money.[7]

To call Larkin a 'Conservative' as Macbeth does, is perhaps mistakenly to align him with the political party that followed the Labour Government of 1964–70 into power. He has certainly never been a socialist. At Oxford, at an age when most young intellectual men are inclined towards socialist principles, Larkin went so far as to have coffee in the University Labour Club's social rooms once or twice, and even to allow Kingsley Amis, then editor of the Club's bulletin, to print a couple of his poems. But, he recalls in his reminiscence of wartime Oxford, which prefaces the second edition of *Jill*, that was the limit of his commitment to the Club's ideology. He is a Conservative, but his kind of conservatism is more like Sir John Betjeman's than Edward Heath's.

This is illustrated by another 'public' poem of Larkin's, which introduced the 1972 H.M.S.O. report, *How Do You Want To Live? A Report on the Human Habitat*. The poem regrets the passing of the England the poet knows, and is informed by the sentiments, though not the sentimentality, of Betjeman's 'The Dear Old Village'. Larkin does not suggest, as Betjeman does, that the

7. 'Homage to a Government', *Sunday Times*, 19 January 1969, p. 60.

masses have abandoned 'old thatch'd cottages' in favour of ugly modern batteries. But he does suggest that 'progress' seems to be destroying more than it creates; that mass-culture is shoddy and tawdry and over-acquisitive; and that a man may be justified in thinking that all England, like Murray Posh and Lupin Pooter in Betjeman's 'Middlesex', will soon be 'silent under soot and stone'. Though the poem is public, Larkin does not claim any vatic authority for his pronouncements. Perhaps, he reflects, his increasing pessimism is due to his growing older; perhaps, he admits, he is over-stating the case. Though he cannot help thinking that England will soon be all 'concrete and tyres',

> Most things are never meant.
> This won't be, most likely: but greeds
> And garbage are too thickly strewn
> To be swept up now, or invent
> Excuses that make them all needs.
> I just think it will happen, soon.[8]

Again, Larkin blames avarice for the difficulties, just as he had blamed it for the decimation of the British presence abroad.

'Livings', published in the *Observer* in 1972, again appears to be 'something different'. None of the poems in *The Less Deceived* or in *The Whitsun Weddings*, by far the best known of Larkin's collections, appeared in groups like the three poems that comprise 'Livings'. However, the title poem of *The North Ship* is a group of four lyrics, and in *XX Poems*, the poem published in *The Less Deceived* as 'Dry Point' had been called 'Etching', and was the second of two poems jointly called 'Two Views of Sex'. The other was called 'Oils', and Larkin chose not to reprint it. The poems of 'Livings' are, as the title suggests, about three ways of life, and each poem is written in a radically different style from the other two. The three poems are dramatic, each creating a different person, as well as a different profession. The first is a small businessman, who deals 'with farmers, things like dips and feed', staying in a commercial hotel. He is a man settling into middle-age; that age, as Larkin says in 'The Building', 'that

8. Prologue, in *How Do You Want to Live? A Report on the Human Habitat*, London 1972, pp. x–xi.

claims/The end of choice, the last of hope'. He is confused about his life, realising that he has no compulsion to carry on his business, other than that 'Father used to'. His life is a meaningless, repetitive round, like the daily papers: 'Births, deaths. For sale. Police court. Motor spares.' His style is appropriately flat and prosaic; even when he describes a beautiful sunset—his description tells us enough to know what sort of sunset it is—his language suggests the numbness of his response:

> a big sky
> Drains down the estuary like the bed
> Of a gold river, and the Customs House
> Still has its office lit.[9]

Besides being about different livings, the poems are set in different times. The first is set in 1929, as its final line tells us; the last might be in 1829, to judge by the style and vocabulary. Like Praed's *Poems of Life and Manners*, it is written in very rhythmic tetrameters, the jingle emphasised by the regular alternation of feminine and masculine rhymes. It is spoken by a young Oxford don—a reference to 'the wood from Snape' indicates that the setting is Oxford rather than Cambridge—who describes the events of an evening, which is like most others except for the fact that the Master of the college is not at dinner. The events are in fact much like those of the first poem: the chit-chat is dull— academic, as uninteresting as the commercial conversation of 'Clough, Margetts, the Captain, Dr Watterson'. This speaker feels constrained to be more poetic about the evening than the first:

> Above, Chaldean constellations
> Sparkle over crowded roofs.

Individually, these two parts may not be surprising to those familiar with Larkin's work. Many of the mature poems create a character in the manner of the first, though the dramatisation is often slightly mocking: 'Self's the Man' is an example. The third part has affinities with 'Naturally the Foundation Will Bear Your Expenses' in satirising the smartness of a young academic. But the second part looks puzzling at first:

9. 'Livings', *Observer*, 20 February 1972, p. 28.

> Keep it all off!
> By night, snow swerves
> (O loose moth world)
> Through the stare travelling
> Leather-black waters.

It is a poem of exhilaration in being part of a wild and stormy night. The speaker is a seaman of some kind, who in no way resents the comfort of inns on shore, where men are protected against the weather. Though this new poem is technically much more competent, and less dependent on stock metaphors and similes than those of Larkin's first book, we must look to *The North Ship* to find a parallel. Here is the first stanza from '75°N. Blizzard', the third of the four connected poems that together form the title poem of *The North Ship*:

> Suddenly clouds of snow
> Begin assaulting the air,
> As falling, as tangled
> As a girl's thick hair.[10]

Larkin's comparison of a snow storm to a cloud of moths in 'Livings' is much more striking, and much more sensuously accurate than this one, which seems to come from Yeats's early poetry, so often draped with the hair of the girl who is the poet's inspiration.

Though Larkin has begun to write different kinds of poems, he has not abandoned his familiar modes. He has written several short poems in the manner of 'Home Is So Sad', poems that capture the mood of a particular moment. Lately, however, these poems have been stimulated by natural observations, rather than domestic ones. 'The Trees' suggests that though trees seem each spring to whisper onomatopoeically 'Begin afresh, afresh, afresh', we should not be fooled into thinking that while we age, natural objects renew themselves yearly. Inside the trunk of each tree, the rings record its growth, and a ring is added every year. Though the trees are free from what Larkin called as early as *A Girl In Winter* 'the caricaturing effects of age', they are not free from the

10. *T.N.S.*, p. 46.

mortality that dogs all natural things; for us and the trees alike,
there is a sense in which, as Larkin says in 'Nothing To Be Said',
'Life is slow dying'.

'Cut Grass' is about natural mortality, too. On a beautiful
summer day, the scent of new-mown grass makes creation seem
perfect—until we remember that what we smell is a dying breath.
The feeling is similar to that in a characteristic sonnet of Robert
Frost, 'The Oven Bird'. Though the bird sings at mid-summer,

> The question that he frames in all but words
> Is what to make of a diminished thing.[11]

Even the height of summer is a decline from spring.

Two poems have appeared that are like 'Church Going' in
style. Like 'Church Going', 'To the Sea' is a poem about the
continuation of tradition, although here Larkin takes as an
instance of the continuation of an attitude the population's
annual trip to the seaside. As far back as the poet can remember,
since his boyhood, these visits have been 'Half an annual pleasure,
half a rite'. The last word suggests a link with sun worship, which
is buried deep in our history and in our consciousness. The visit
to the sea, with aged parents and young children, is as 'serious' as
the visit to the church made by the speaker in 'Church Going'.
And if the perfect weather highlights our imperfections, the fulfilment of our duties and responsibilities towards old and young
may in some way compensate.

>   If the worst
> Of flawless weather is our falling short,
> It may be that through habit these do best,
> Coming to water clumsily undressed
> Yearly; teaching their children by a sort
> Of clowning; helping the old, too, as they ought.[12]

Like 'Church Going', the poem works through from a rather
dismissive attitude, to the speaker's recognition of the real

11. *The Poetry of Robert Frost*, ed. Edward Connery Lathem, London 1971,
p. 120.
12. 'To the Sea', *London Magazine*, IX (January 1970), p. 29.

PHILIP LARKIN

importance of what he is observing. The change from second
person to third, 'our' to 'they', is not patronising; it is the
reverse: Larkin recognises that these rather ordinary, unthinking
people are in one respect more fully responsible than he is. The
poem may further explain Larkin's attitudes in 'Homage to a
Government' and the poem that introduced *How Do You Want
To Live?*: 'To the Sea' expresses keen concern about the fulfilment
of duties in private life. These other poems, on political issues,
express the extension of that concern into public affairs.

In some respects, 'The Building'[13] is reminiscent more of 'I
Remember, I Remember' than of 'Church Going'. Like 'I
Remember, I Remember', it has a very complex rhyme scheme
that cuts across stanza breaks. It has eight-line rhyme units, each
unit being rhymed abcbdcad, and the final line, typographically
separate from the rest of the poem, completes the form. But in fact,
'The Building' is a sort of ' "Church Going" Revisited'. It is
almost the same length as the earlier poem: where 'Church
Going' had seven nine-line stanzas, 'The Building' has nine
seven-line stanzas, plus a single final line. The building in question
is a hospital, certainly a 'serious' place, a place 'proper to grow
wise in'. It has much to do with birth, and more with death;
though it is not so much the dead who 'lie round' here as those
about to die: 'The unseen congregations whose white rows/Lie
set apart above'. In 'Church Going' the speaker goes to a church
to cure a 'hunger', though at first he does not realise what is
wrong with him; similarly, people go to the hospital looking for a
cure in the knowledge that something is wrong, though unsure
exactly what it is.

Larkin's metaphors make links between the hospital and the
church: the patients are an 'unseen congregation', people go to the
hospital to 'confess', and visitors bring 'wasteful, weak, propitia-
tory flowers', like those 'flowers, cut/For Sunday, brownish now'
of 'Church Going'. The hospital is a sort of secular substitute for
the failed church. From the window, the speaker can see 'a
locked church', suggesting a religious creed that can no longer
command assent; and at the end of the poem, the speaker says that
the building tries to 'outbuild cathedrals' for they had proved too
low to act as a bulwark against our horror of 'the coming dark'.

13. 'The Building', *New Statesman*, 17 March 1972, p. 356.

Larkin grows more pessimistic as he ages. Speaking to Ian Hamilton about 'Church Going' he said that when birth, marriage and death 'are dispersed into the registry office and the crematorium chapel life will become thinner in consequence.'[14] 'The Building' shows that he believes this has happened. The church first, then the rest of the country, perhaps: 'I just think it will happen, soon.'

Though he may be justified in this pessimism, he is less justified in his pessimism about his own future. When he introduced his poem 'The Explosion' in the radio broadcast that marked his fiftieth birthday, he said: 'I doubt if writers get any better after they're fifty, and I don't suppose I shall be any exception.' Happily, there *are* many exceptions to this rule. Hardy wrote his best poems in his seventies; Yeats was forty-nine before he began to draw himself, with *Responsibilities*, up to his full stature as a poet, and sixty-two when *The Tower* was published in 1928; some would consider Eliot's greatest achievement to be *Four Quartets*, and the first quartet, 'Burnt Norton', was published when the poet was fifty-one. The poems I have discussed in this chapter indicate that Larkin has not reached a dead end, and 'The Building' in particular shows that his powers are undiminished.

I am sure that Larkin will continue to produce fine poems, which will reach a wide readership. Both things are important: as C. K. Stead argues in his excellent study of modern poetry, *The New Poetic: Yeats to Eliot*, poetry is in its healthiest state when the poet has an ideal relationship with both reality and his audience. If we see the relationship between poet, reality and audience as three points of a triangle, Stead says, 'the finest poems in any language are likely to be those which exist in an equilateral triangle, each point pulling perfectly in a moment of perfect tension.'[15] A poet may distort the triangle by losing touch with his readers or with life, but I believe that many of Larkin's poems achieve this 'perfect tension': he is a poet who compromises neither reality nor his audience.

14. 'Four Conversations', p. 74.
15. C. K. Stead, *The New Poetic: Yeats to Eliot*, Harmondsworth 1967, p. 12.

Select Bibliography

1   Philip Larkin

1. *Books* (All editions cited in the text are included in this section, and indicated by an asterisk.)

The North Ship. London (The Fortune Press) 1945. 2nd edition, introduced, and with an additional poem taken from *XX Poems*, by Philip Larkin, London (Faber) 1966.*

Jill. London (The Fortune Press) 1946. 2nd edition, introduced by Philip Larkin, London (Faber) 1964.*

A Girl in Winter. London (Faber) 1947, 1956, 1965.*

XX Poems. Privately printed in a limited edition of 100. Thirteen of the twenty poems later appeared in *The Less Deceived*. Another was added to the second edition of *The North Ship*. Belfast, 1951.

Fantasy Press: Pamphlet 21. All five of the poems in this pamphlet appeared in *The Less Deceived*. Swinford, 1954.

The Less Deceived. Hessle, Yorkshire (The Marvell Press) 1955, 6th impression, 1966.*

The Whitsun Weddings. London (Faber) 1964, 4th impression, 1968.*

All What Jazz: A Record Diary 1961–68. London (Faber) 1970.

2. *Uncollected Poems*

'Tops', in *Listen*, II (Spring 1957), p. 6.

'Success Story', in *Beloit Poetry Journal*, VIII (Winter 1957–8), p. 36.

'Breadfruit', in *Critical Quarterly*, III (Winter 1961), p. 309.

'Love', in *Critical Quarterly*, VIII (Summer 1966), p. 173.

'How Distant', in *Listener*, 28 October 1967, p. 521.

'Sympathy in White Major', in *London Magazine*, VII (December 1967), p. 13.

'The Trees', in *New Statesman*, 17 May 1968, p. 659.

'High Windows', in *Word in the Desert: Critical Quarterly Tenth Anniversary Number*, (Spring–Summer 1968), p. 55.

'Posterity', in *New Stateman*, 28 June 1968, p. 876.

'Sad Steps', in *New Statesman*, 28 June 1968, p. 876.

'Homage to a Government', in *Sunday Times*, 19 January 1969, p. 60.

'A Couplet by Philip Larkin', in *Black Paper II: The Crisis in Education*, ed. C. B. Cox and A. E. Dyson, London 1969, p. 133.

'Annus Mirabilis', in *London Magazine*, IX (January 1970), p. 29.

'To the Sea', in *London Magazine*, IX (January 1970), pp. 28–9.

'The Card Players', in *Encounter*, XXXV (October 1970), p. 41.

'Dublinesque', in *Encounter*, XXXV (October 1970), p. 41.

'Vers de Société', in *New Statesman*, 18 June 1971, p. 854.

'Cut Grass', in *Listener*, 29 July 1971, p. 144.

'Livings', in *Observer*, 20 February 1972, p. 28.

'The Building', in *New Statesman*, 17 March 1972, p. 356.

'Heads in the Woman's Ward', in *New Humanist*, I (May 1972), p. 17.

'Prologue', in *How Do You Want to Live? A Report on the Human Habitat*, London (H.M.S.O.) 1972, pp. x–xi.

'The Explosion', in *Listener*, 17 August 1972, p. 208.

3. *Uncollected Prose Pieces*

'No More Fever', in *Listen*, II (Summer 1956), pp. 22–6.

'The Writer in His Age: Philip Larkin', in *London Magazine*, IV (May 1957), pp. 46–7.

'The Pleasure Principle', in *Listen*, II (Summer–Autumn 1957), pp. 28–32.

'No Fun Any More', in *Manchester Guardian*, 18 November 1958, p. 4.

'Betjeman en Bloc', *Listen*, III (Spring 1959), pp. 14–22.

'Not the Place's Fault', in *Umbrella*, I (Summer 1959), pp. 107–12.

'Savage Seventh', in *Spectator*, 20 November 1959, pp. 713–14.

'John Press, *Guy Fawkes Night and Other Poems*', in *Critical Quarterly*, I (Winter 1959), pp. 362–3.

'What's Become of Wystan?' in *Spectator*, 15 July 1960, pp. 104–5.

'The Blending of Betjeman', in *Spectator*, 2 December 1960, p. 913.

'Masters' Voices', in *New Statesman*, 2 February 1962, pp. 170–1.
'Context: Philip Larkin', in *London Magazine*, I (February 1962), pp. 31–2.
'Mrs Hardy's Memories', in *Critical Quarterly*, IV (Spring 1962), pp. 75–9.
'The Poetry of William Barnes', in *Listener*, 16 August 1962, p. 257.
'Frivolous and Vulnerable', in *New Statesman*, 28 September 1962, pp. 416, 418.
'Absences', in *Poet's Choice*, ed. Paul Engel and Joseph Langland, New York (New Directions) 1962, pp. 202–3.
'The War Poet', in *Listener*, 10 October 1963, pp. 561–2.
'*Christina Rossetti*, Lona Mosk Packer; *The Rossetti–Macmillan Letters*, ed. Lona Mosk Packer', in *Listener*, 26 March 1964, p. 526.
'Wanted: Good Hardy Critic', in *Critical Quarterly*, VIII (Summer 1966), pp. 174–9.
'Operation Manuscript', in *Poetry in the Making: A Catalogue of an Exhibition of Poetry Manuscripts in the British Museum, April–June 1967*, ed. Jenny Lewis, London (Turret Books) 1967, pp. 14–21.
'The Apollo Bit', in *New Statesman*, 14 June 1968, pp. 798, 799, 802.
'Philip Larkin Praises the Poetry of Thomas Hardy', in *Listener*, 25 July 1968, p. 111.
'The Most Victorian Laureate', in *New Statesman*, 14 March 1969, pp. 363–4.
'Big Victims: Emily Dickinson and Walter de la Mare', in *New Statesman*, 13 March 1970, pp. 367–8.
'It could Only Happen in England: A Study of John Betjeman's Poems for American Readers', in *The Cornhill* 1969 (Autumn 1971), pp. 21–36. This essay was published as the Introduction to John Betjeman's *Collected Poems*, enlarged edition, compiled by the Earl of Birkenhead, Boston (Houghton Mifflin) 1971.
'Stevie, Goodbye', in *Observer*, 23 January 1972, p. 28.
'The Hidden Hardy', in *New Statesman*, 2 June 1972, pp. 752–3.
'The State of Poetry—A Symposium: Philip Larkin', in *The Review*, 29–30 (Spring–Summer 1972), p. 60.

3. Edited by Philip Larkin

New Poems, Ed. Philip Larkin, Louis MacNiece and Bonamy Dobree, London (Michael Joseph) 1958.

The Oxford Book of Twentieth-Century English Verse, London (Oxford University Press) 1973.

4. Gramophone Records

'Philip Larkin Reads *The Less Deceived*', Listen Records (LPV 1), 1958, 1968. In the case of the 1958 release, the sleeve note is a publishing history of *The Less Deceived*. In 1968, it is a short interview with Larkin on the subject of reading his poems. Neither piece is reprinted elsewhere.

'Philip Larkin Reads and Comments on *The Whitsun Weddings*', Listen Records (LPV 6), 1965. The sleeve note is Christopher Ricks's excellent review of *The Whitsun Weddings*, from the *New York Review of Books*.

5. Interviews with Philip Larkin

ANON, 'Four Young Poets—I: Philip Larkin', in *Times Educational Supplement*, 13 July 1956, p. 933.
—— 'Speaking of Writing XIII: Philip Larkin', in *Times*, 20 February 1964, p. 16.

HAMILTON, IAN, 'Four Conversations: Philip Larkin', in *London Magazine*, IV (November 1964), pp. 71–7.

HORDER, JOHN, 'Poet on the 8.15', in *Manchester Guardian*, 20 May 1965, p. 9.

HILL, DOUGLAS, 'Poet Who Captures the Music of Daily Life', in *Coventry Evening Telegraph*, 6 October 1972, p. 30.

HILL, FRANCES, 'A Sharp Edged View', in *Times Educational Supplement*, 19 May 1972, p. 19.

OAKES, PHILIP, 'The Unsung Gold Medallist', in *Sunday Times Magazine*, 27 March 1966, pp. 63–5.

II   Others

ALVAREZ, A., 'Poetry of the Fifties in England', in *International Literary Annual No. 1*, ed. John Wain, London 1958, pp. 97–107.

——— (Ed.), *The New Poetry*, 2nd edition, Harmondsworth 1966.

——— 'Philip Larkin', in *Beyond All This Fiddle*, London 1968, pp. 85–7.

ANON, 'In the Movement', in *Spectator*, 1 October 1954, p. 399.

——— 'Poetic Moods', in *Times Literary Supplement*, 16 December 1955, p. 762.

——— 'Undeceived Poet', in *Times Literary Supplement*, 12 March 1964, p. 216.

——— 'A Solitary Sensibility', in *Time*, 19 February 1965, pp. 101–2.

——— 'Out of the Air: Not Like Larkin', in *Listener*, 17 August 1972, p. 209.

BALL, PATRICIA, 'The Photographic Art', in *Review of English Literature*, III (April 1962), pp. 50–8.

BATESON, F. W., 'Auden's (and Empson's) Heirs', in *Essays in Criticism*, VII (January 1957), pp. 76–80.

BELL, WILLIAM (Ed.), *Poetry from Oxford in Wartime*, London 1945.

BERGONZI, BERNARD, 'After the "Movement": English Poetry Today', in *Listener*, 24 August 1961, pp. 284–5.

BETJEMAN, JOHN, 'Common Experiences', in *Listener*, 19 March 1964, p. 483.

BOGAN, LOUISE, 'Books: Verse', in *New Yorker*, 10 April 1965, pp. 193, 194, 196.

CONQUEST, ROBERT (Ed.), *New Lines: An Anthology*, London 1956.
——— *New Lines—II*, London 1963.

COX, C. B., 'Philip Larkin', in *Critical Quarterly* I (Spring 1959), pp. 14–7.
——— and DYSON, A. E. (Eds.), *Modern Poetry: Studies in Practical Criticism*, London 1963.

CRISPIN, EDMUND, 'An Oxford Group', in *Spectator*, 17 April 1964, p. 525.

DAVIE, DONALD, *Purity of Diction in English Verse*, London 1952.

DODSWORTH, MARTIN, 'The Climate of Pain in Recent Poetry', in *London Magazine*, IV (November 1964), pp. 86–95.

ENRIGHT, D. J., 'Down Cemetery Road', in *New Statesman*, 28 February 1964, pp. 331–1.
——— (Ed.), *Poets of the 1950's: An Anthology of New English Verse*, Tokyo 1955.

FALCK, COLIN, 'The Whitsun Weddings', in *The Review*, XIV (December 1964), pp. 3–11.

FRASER, G. S. and FLETCHER, IAIN, *Springtime: An Anthology o Young Poets*, London 1953.

FRASER, G. S., *Poetry Now: An Anthology*, London 1956.

—— *Vision and Rhetoric: Studies in Modern Poetry*, London 1959.

—— and OTHERS, 'English Poetry Since 1945', in *London Magazine*, VI (November 1959), pp. 11–36.

—— *The Modern Writer and His World*, revised ed., with epilogue, Harmondsworth 1970.

GARDNER, P., 'The Wintry Drum: the Poetry of Philip Larkin', in *Dalhousie Reviews*, XLVIII (Spring 1968), pp. 88–99.

GINDIN, JAMES, *Postwar British Fiction: New Accents and Attitudes*, London 1962.

GRUBB, FREDERICK, 'No One Actually Starves: Philip Larkin', in *A Vision of Reality: A Study of Liberalism in Twentieth Century Verse*, London 1965, pp. 226–35.

HAMILTON, IAN, '*The Whitsun Weddings*', in *London Magazine*, IV (May 1964), pp. 70–4.

HOBSBAUM, PHILIP, 'Where Are the War Poets?' in *Outposts*, 61 (Summer 1964), pp. 21–3.

HOLLOWAY, JOHN, 'New Lines in English Poetry', in *Hudson Review*, IX (Winter 1956–7), pp. 592–7.

HOPE, FRANCIS, 'Philip Larkin', in *Encounter*, XXII (May 1964), pp. 72–4.

JENNINGS, ELIZABETH, 'The Larkin Tone', in *Spectator*, 23 September 1966, pp. 385–6.

JONES, A. R., 'The Poetry of Philip Larkin: A Note on Transatlantic Culture', in *Western Humanities Review*, XVI (Spring 1962), pp. 143–52.

LEHMANN, JOHN, 'The Wain-Larkin Myth: A Reply to John Wain', in *Sewanee Review*, 66 (Fall 1958), pp. 578–87.

O'CONNOR, WILLIAM VAN, *The New University Wits*, Carbondale 1963.

PARKINSON, R. N., ' "To Keep Our Metaphysics Warm": A Study of 'Church Going" by Philip Larkin', in *The Critical Survey*, V (Winter 1971), pp. 224–33.

PRESS, JOHN, 'English Verse Since 1945', in *Essays by Divers Hands*, XXXI, London 1962, pp. 143–84.
―――― *Rule and Energy: Trends in British Poetry Since the Second World War*, London 1963.

RICKS, CHRISTOPHER, 'A True Poet', in *New York Review of Books*, 28 January 1965, pp. 10–1.

ROSENTHAL, M. L., 'Tuning in on Albion', in *The Nation*, 16 May 1959, pp. 457–9.

SCARFE, FRANCIS, *Auden and After: The Liberation of Poetry 1930–41*, London 1942.

SWINDEN, PATRICK, 'Old Lines, New Lines: The Movement Ten Years After', in *Critical Quarterly*, IX (Winter 1967), pp. 347–59.

THWAITE, ANTHONY, 'The Poetry of Philip Larkin', in *The Survival of Poetry: A Contemporary Survey*, ed. Martin Dodsworth, London 1970, pp. 37–55.

TOMLINSON, CHARLES, 'The Middlebrow Muse', in *Essays in Criticism*, VII (January 1957), pp. 208–17.
―――― 'Poetry Today', in *The Pelican Guide to English Literature: 7, The Modern Age*, ed. Boris Ford, 2nd edition, Harmondsworth 1964, pp. 458–74.

WAIN, JOHN, 'English Poetry: The Immediate Situation', in *Sewanee Review*, LXV (Summer 1957), pp. 353–74.
―――― 'Engagement or Withdrawal? Some Notes on the Work of Philip Larkin', in *Critical Quarterly*, VI (Summer 1964), pp. 167–78.
―――― *Sprightly Running*, London 1965.

WEATHERHEAD, A. KINGSLEY, 'Philip Larkin of England', in *ELH* XXXVIII (December 1971), pp. 616–30.